Amazon -

to Buy or Not to Buy

Eric Thomsen

2023

Amazon – to Buy or Not to Buy

Eric Thomsen

ISBN **978-1-960269-36-2**

Contact the author and publishers at editionslux2015@gmail.com

Cover: Jeff Bezos´ iconic laugh Steve Jurvetson

Inside 1: Jeff Bezoos visits the Los Angeles Air Force base, Space and Missile Systems center and spoke to the Commanders and Leaderships of Air Force Space Command at Ft. MacArthur, San Pedro, Calif., Oct 25, 2017 (cropped). Image: OptimusPrimeBot
Rear: Demonstrators supporting union rights Myotus

Other titles by the author

Tesla

Hybrid Future

Catalonia – Way to Conflict

Jamal Kashoggi – What is the Problem?

Arab Oil Money – Toxic Cocktail

Radical Islam and Compliance in Financial Institutions

Hezbollah – Cuckoo in the Nest

Clinton Stories – series

Luxembourg Wealth Management - series

Compliance - series

Huawei executive Meng Wanzhou case Vol 1 &2

Trump Lied!

Compliance: Biden

Obama Betrayed America

About the author

Eric Thomsen has published in law, science and economics. He holds several law degrees, a degree in economics and was ACAMS certified in 2016.

Content

Note:

The pixilated pictures in this book are thumbnails on the internet and not really intended for a print book version.

Introduction

The question – to buy or not to buy – is eternal.

It does not matter whether it is Amazon stock (AMZN) or products from Amazon – it is still an eternal question. It is a basic human question.

We will take you on a tantalizing journey through 16 books available on Amazon Books.

Each click has new fascinating revelations – new worlds and world views open all the time – but at the end of the day the question still remains –

To buy or not to buy.

The Issue

‴

Eric Thomsen <editionslux2015@gmail.com> 05.01 (for 2 timer siden)

til amazon-ir

Board of Directors

Amazon.com Inc

It has come to our attention that Amazon has been selling our books for the last abt two years without paying author´s fees.

The books you have been selling have ISBN numbers for versions uploaded to Ingram (Ingram Industries Inc). There are 291 titles.

We ask you please to provide sales data and we request a prompt settlement of the authors fees accrued, using the formula by Ingram.

We have contacted Amazon Head Office several times without response and we are taking steps to pursue the issue.

Systematic production and selling counterfeit goods covered by copyright is a criminal offense in most jurisdiction.

We hope for a speedy resolution of the issue.

Sincerely,

Eric Thomsen and Cristina Berna"

Email sent to Amazon.com Inc Board of Directors to an email address obtained from

https://ir.aboutamazon.com/officers-and-directors/default.aspx

Copyright statement

The standard copyright statement which is typically found on page 2 in every one of our books, above the ISBN number.....

Facts and allegations

We start in Spain – in lovely vibrant Sevilla baked by the Andalucian sun. Here flamenco dancers mesmerize onlookers to enchanting gipsy guitars while the rich bouquet of the Andalucian red wine pearl your palet.

We uploaded 16 books from 7 Oct 2022 to 28 Dec 2022 to our new Spanish agent.

We will take you on a journey through Amazon Books in their websites following these titles as they develop – click by click.

Since then and until the time of writing we have uploaded 20 more books and we may take that journey later.

Joaquin Sorolla: *Sevilla. El baile*, gouache, Museo Sorolla, Madrid. Study for a painting in 1915 in Hispanic Society of America, New York Image : Szilas

The first 16 books uploaded via our agent are:

Página 2 de 2, mostrando 16 de **36 resultados**, empezando en 21, terminando en 36

Joaquín Sorolla Family

Cristina Berna

Precio: 79.95€

ISBN: 978-1-960269-01-0

"Precio" is price in Spanish. "ISBN" is a unique number each title has, like a chassis number on a car. ISBN stands for International Standard Book Number. It gives the title and the author.

Joaquín Sorolla Beach

Cristina Berna Precio 49.95€ ISBN 978-1-960269-00-3

Hiroshige Famous Views of the Sixty-odd Provinces

Cristina Berna Precio 99.95€ ISBN 978-1-956773-99-6

Hiroshige Kunisada Kuniyoshi 53 Pairings of the Tokaido

Cristina Berna Precio 99.95€ ISBN 978-1-956773-97-2

Hokusai 36 Views of Mt Fuji

Cristina Berna Precio 99.95€ ISBN 978-1-956773-98-9

Keisai Eisen A Tōkado Board Game of Courtesans

Cristina Berna Precio 149.95€ ISBN 978-1-956773-92-7

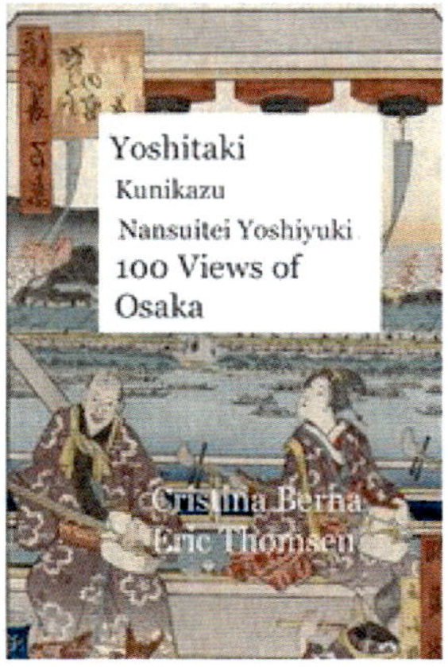

Yoshitaki Kunikazu Nsuitei Yoshiyuki 100 Views of Osaka

Cristina Berna Precio 99.95€I SBN 978-1-956773-96-5

Hiroshige 100 Famous Views of Edo

Cristina Berna Precio 99.95€ ISBN 978-1-956773-95-8

Cats in Art Timeline

Cristina Berna Precio 79.95€ ISBN 978-1-956773-94-1

Joaquín Sorolla Nudes

Cristina Berna Precio 79.95€ ISBN 978-1-956773-93-4

Joaquín Sorolla Desnudos

Cristina Berna Precio 79.95€ ISBN 9781956773903

Joaquin Sorolla Playa

Cristina Berna Precio 79.95€ ISBN 978-1-956773-8-80

Gatos en el arte

Cristina Berna Precio 99.95€ ISBN 978-1-956773-84-2

Hiroshige 36 Vistas de Monte Fuji 1858

Cristina Berna Precio 79.95€ ISBN 978-1-956773-83-5

Hiroshige 36 Vistas de Monte Fuji 1852

Cristina Berna Precio 79.95€ ISBN 978-1-956773-81-1

Luxemburgo - un pedazo de tarta

Berna Cristina Precio 49.95€ ISBN 978-1-956773-23-1

Just a small note : The thumbnail for "Joaquin Sorolla Playa" is missing in our agent´s display so we borrowed the picture from the English version above. Some of our books are in Spanish, most in English and a few is even in German, French, Chinese, Danish or other language.

The strange sign € after the price means Euro – it is more or less the same as a $.

Now we will look carefully at each book and we will start with the first uploaded.

[*Luxemburgo - un pedaza de tarta*]

Berna Cristina Precio 49.95€ ISBN 978-1-956773-23-1

We wrote this little book as a tribute to Luxembourg, with all the fond memories we have from living in Luxembourg city. We especially enjoyed the superb cakes. It is one of the best places in Europe to sample cakes.

The book is published in English, Danish, French, German, Spanish, Italian and Portuguese......all on Ingram (Lightning Spark, Ingram Industries Inc, Tennessee), and Ingram "cancelled" the book for no good reason on and about July 2021 as an abuse of their near monopoly contractual hold over independent bookstores World Wide, something which should be against EU and probably also US anti-trust law.

From Oct 2022 the authors started to re-publish some of these "cancelled" books via our new agent, a Spanish publisher that according to their own statement "do not discriminate against books".

Amazon has not yet included this book on their website which they should have done according to our agent.

Our agent answered a query 4 April 2023:

"We are only aggregators of El Corte Ingles, FNAC, Amazon, Casa del Libro ...".

An author+title specific search on amazon.com yielded this result:

"No results for cristina berna luxembourgo.

Use fewer keywords or try these instead
No results for cristina berna luxembourgo in Books.

NEED HELP?"

The search link was:

https://www.amazon.com/s?k=cristina+berna+luxembourgo&crid=1T5HIYTBJLGDG&sprefix=cristina+berna+luxembourgo+%2Caps%2C381&ref=nb_sb_noss

If you narrow the search on amazon to "cristina berna luxembourg" you get this result:

Luxembourg - Ren Kage: Nyd Luxembourg og dets kager (Danish Edition)

Danish Edition | by Cristina Berna and Eric Thomsen | Mar 25, 2019

No reviews

Paperback

$5.26 $5.26

List: $49.95 $49.95

Delivery **Tue, Apr 18**

Ships to Austria

Only 1 left in stock - order soon.

Luxembourg - un morceau de gâteau: L'échantillonnage du Luxembourg et de ses gâteaux, avec ses propres photos: Hardcover (French Edition)

French Edition | by Cristina Berna and Eric Thomsen | Mar 18, 2019

No reviews

Hardcover

Paperback

$4.55 $4.55

List: $29.95 $29.95

Delivery **Mon, Apr 24**

Or fastest delivery **Wed, Apr 12**

Ships to Austria

Only 1 left in stock - order soon.

卢森堡 - 一块蛋糕 抽样卢森堡及其蛋糕 插图: Luxembourg - a piece of cake (Chinese Edition)

Chinese Edition | by Cristina Berna and Eric Thomsen | Feb 18, 2019

No reviews

Hardcover

5.24 5.24

List: $49.95 $49.95

Delivery **Thu, Apr 20**

Or fastest delivery **Thu, Apr 13**

Ships to Austria

Only 1 left in stock - order soon.

Paperback

The link for the search was:

https://www.amazon.com/s?k=cristina+berna+luxembourg&i=stripbooks-intl-ship&crid=LZLRN6QA0KM1&sprefix=cristina+berna+luxembourg%2Cstripbooks-intl-ship%2C413&ref=nb_sb_noss

These books are all formally “unavailable” ....they have been “cancelled” by Ingram (Ingram´s own term) on or about July 2021. Officially no copies have been printed since then.

You see Amazon is offering these titles at a price far below list price €49.95.

For the French Ingram-version the paperback price is:

Paperback

$4.55 $4.55

List: $29.95 $29.95

How is it possible for Amazon to offer our book for sale at $4.55? And how can Amazon do that when the list price issued to Ingram was $29.95?

Again, how can Amazon offer this title for sale for €4.55 when the list price issued through Ingram is €29.95?

This price hardly covers printing, and is above what we must pay for the Spanish version to have it printed with our new agent.

The Chinese version is offered for sale by Amazon at:

[Hardcover]

5.24 5.24

List: $49.95 $49.95

The hardback version only cost $0.69 or €0.69 more for a hardcover version compared by the $4.55/€4.55 for a paperback – although in French.

These are extremely attractive prices.

It is incredible that Amazon is offering books for sale at such bargain prices.

These are so low prices that few potential buyers would be able to resist if price is the deciding factor for buying "entertainment" or "content".

Let us move on to the second book.

[Hiroshige 36 Vistas de Monte Fuji 1852]

Cristina Berna Precio 79.95€ ISBN 978-1-956773-81-1

The second book we uploaded to our agent, *Hiroshige 36 Vistas de Monte Fuji 1858*.

This title was uploaded 9 Nov 2022.

Our agent is showing us (in our internal system) a link to the book´s page in amazon.es

Plataforma	Enlace
ama	https://www.amazon.es/s/ref=nb_sb_noss?__mk_es_ES=%C3%85M%C3%85%C5%BD%C3%95%C3%91&url=search-alias%3Daps&field-keywords=9781956773811

but when you click this link you get this result (as of 6 April 2023):

«No hay resultados para 9781956773811.

El precio y otros detalles pueden variar en función del tamaño y el color del producto. »

"Utilice menos palabras clave o pruebe con estas«

Translated :

"*No results for 9781956773811.*

The price and other details may vary depending on the size and color of the product

Use fewer keywords or try these"...

Compared to our first book uploaded on our agent, where there was no link at all to a book page with amazon.es we are one step up here – we have a link, but it does not produce anything.

What does this mean?

We saw under the first book that our agent distributed to Amazon, but there was no link to a book page for the particular book version.

There was however out on amazon.com in general search results – not to the Spanish version, but to other language versions which have been "cancelled" by Ingram abt two years ago, but are apparently still on sale with amazon.com

These other "cancelled" language versions are indeed on "sale" – they are offered by Amazon.com at rock-bottom prices that do not cover even the printing costs we are charged by our agent for the Spanish version.

What happens if w(e do a general search on amazon.com but author+title specific?

The search link (6 Apr 2023) is:

https://www.amazon.de/s?k=cristina+berna+Hiroshige+36+Vistas+de+Monte+Fuji+1852&crid=2TG0LH4VBZOSZ&sprefix=cristina+berna+hiroshige+36+vistas+de+monte+fuji+1852%2Caps%2C151&ref=nb_sb_noss

one result for **"cristina berna Hiroshige 36 Vistas de Monte Fuji 1852"**

RESULTS…

Hiroshige 36 Vistas de Monte Fuji 1852: Premium

Spanish edition | by Cristina Berna and Eric Thomsen | 7 Mar 2020

No reviews

Hardcover

Currently unavailable.

Amazon.com states the title is unavailable.

If you click on the title, you get the following information:

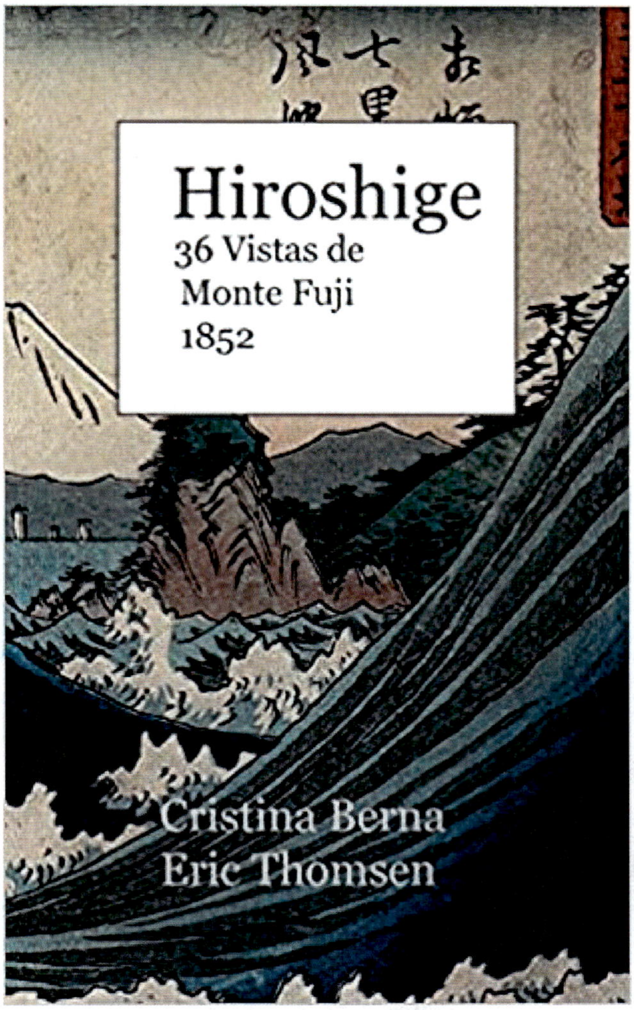
Hiroshige
36 Vistas de
Monte Fuji
1852
Cristina Berna
Eric Thomsen

Hiroshige 36 Vistas de Monte Fuji 1852: Premium Hardcover – Illustrated, 7 Mar. 2020

Spanish edition by Cristina Berna (Autor), Eric Thomsen (Autor)

No reviews

See all formats and editions

- **Hardcover**
  —

...

Product details

- **Publisher :** Missys Clan; Illustrated edition (7 Mar. 2020)
- **Language :** Spanish
- **Hardcover :** 112 pages
- **ISBN-10 :** 1647862884
- **ISBN-13 :** 978-1647862886
- **Dimensions :** 15.24 x 1.12 x 22.86 cm

You see this is a different, older version, and it is hardcover.

It was published by Ingram for us 7 Mar 2020 and "cancelled" on or about July 2021. As Amazon states, it is, so to say, "unavailable". From Ingram, it should be.

The ISBN number for this version is 978-1-647862-88-6.

This is a unique international standard book number we purchased from ISBN Services Inc in New York.

But note the other link here:

See all formats and editions

What does this mean?

Is there perhaps a link to our book version uploaded to our agent 9 Nov 2022?

Here is the drop-down we got, which does not display a specific link:

- (2)

Hiroshige 36 Vistas de Monte Fuji 1852

€62.19 €62.19

New from €60.50

Rating	(0)
ISBN-13	**978-1647863142**

Hiroshige 36 Vistas de Monte Fuji 1852: Premium

-

Rating	(0)
ISBN-13	**978-1647862886**
Publisher	Missys Clan
Edition	Illustrated
Publication Date	7 Mar. 2020

- ←Previous
- 1
- Next→

You note the second book on the drop down is listed with ISBN **978-1647862886** which is the same number as the hardcopy in the search result.

You note it is shown to be "Premium" i.e. the best quality offered by Ingram in terms of paper and color of the print.

You also note another ISBN number, **978-1-647883-14-2**, which is the number for the paperback version uploaded to Ingram 7 Mar 2020.

Maybe you also note the small discrete link there.

New from €60.50

We click on it to see, if we get to the version we uploaded 9 Nov 2022 to our agent.

But, no.

Instead opens another drop down with the following information:

_Back to all formats and editions

Hiroshige 36 Vistas de Monte Fuji 1852
Hardcover

New
€62.19 €62.19

FREE delivery **Saturday, April 15**

Or fastest delivery **Wednesday, April 12**. Order within 9 hrs 50 mins

Submit Add to Basket

Dispatches from

Amazon

Sold by

Amazon
Return policy

See less

FREE delivery **Saturday, April 15**

Or fastest delivery **Wednesday, April 12**. Order within 9 hrs 50 mins

---

1 other option
sorted by price + delivery: low to high

Filter (1)

New

Clear all

New
€134.68 €134.68

€5.69 delivery **April 26 - May 19**. Details

Submit Add to Basket

Dispatches from

Bigly Books.

Sold by

Bigly Books.

(25 ratings)
89% positive over last 12 months

Return policy

End of results

But, what is this?

You see Amazon as Amazon is offering for sale a title that was “cancelled “abt two years ago – not by us but by Ingram – and Amazon is offering it at a price of €62.19.

Recall that our newly uploaded version, which Amazon does not give a link to, although they show our agent that the book has a link and is offered at €79.95.

Amazon is selling an “unavailable” title for €17.76 less than we sell our book through our agent for.

How can Amazon get an “unavailable” book and offer that for sale? And sell it cheaper than our agent´s version?

What we are especially concerned about is that Amazon is not providing any sales data to us.

We have asked Amazon for the sales data.

Amazon has not replied.

Why we are concerned about the lack of sales data is because we are supposed to be paid an author´s fee, a royalty, be paid the fruits of our labor.

We live from writing books.

It sure looks like Amazon has been selling this "unavailable" title for two years now, without giving us any sales data and without paying us any author´s fees.

That is a good reason to ask Amazon, where they got this book from.

We have asked Amazon kindly to produce an invoice for the purchase of this book.

Amazon has not replied.

It looks Amazon is price dumping us.

Actually it is extremely difficult to get through to Amazon unless you want to buy something.

But what is the other information in this "drop down" inside a "drop down"?

There is another seller called:
Bigly Books.

And this seller is offering the "unavailable" book for a whopping €134.68.

That is €54.73 more than we are offering our book for via our agent.

Bigly Books also do not send us any sales data and Bigly Books also do not pay us any author´s fees.

Where does Bigly Books get the "unavailable" version "cancelled" by Ingram abt two years ago from?

We click on the link and get this result:

Bigly Books has a link inside the amazon.com system:

https://www.amazon.de/sp?language=en&ie=UTF8&seller=A1O0VK1TEW3Z0P&isAmazonFulfilled=0&asin=1647863147&ref_=olp_merch_name_1

From the link we copy the following information:

Detailed Seller Information
Business seller

Business Name: BIGLY BOOKS LTD

Business Type: Privately-owned business

Trade Register Number: SC646707

Business Address:

Westpoint

4 Redheughs Rigg

EDINBURGH

EDINBURGH

EH12 9DQ

GB

On the Bigly Books website inside Amazon.com is the possibility for asking a question:

Have a question for Bigly Books.?

Ask a question

We submit, again, the following question to Bigly Books:

"Dear Sirs, where do you get our book ISBN 978-1647863142 *Hiroshige 36 Vistas de Monte Fuji 1852* from? Would you be as kind and give us a copy of the invoice? Sincerely, Cristina Berna and Eric Thomsen, copyright holders"

We will see what they answer. It was an automated service that offered two other of our "cancelled" titles for sale.

On Bigly Books website inside amazon.com is a "storefront".

Bigly Books.

Visit the Bigly Books. storefront

*4.5 out of 5 stars***89% positive** in the last 12 months (18 ratings)

If you click that, you get on this link:

https://www.amazon.de/s?me=A1O0VK1TEW3Z0P&language=en&marketplaceID=A1PA6795UKMFR9

1-16 of over 100,000 results

Here is webpage after webpage with books that Bigly Books is offering for sale.

Bigly Books is one of Amazon´s "trusted sellers". They work together under the amazon umbrella to sell stuff.

You can search the amazon main webpage, but via BIGLY BOOKS, which is displayed now to the left in the search bar, where you usually have all the Amazon departments...

we enter author name "Cristina Berna"....and we get the following result:

10 results for **"Cristina Berna"**

Sort by: Featured Sort by:Featured

RESULTS

Learn about these results.

Missy's Clan - Education

English edition | by Cristina Berna and Eric Thomsen

No reviews

Paperback

€16.23 €16.23

Get it **Tuesday, 2 May** - **Wednesday, 24 May**

€5.54 delivery

Christmas Market Malaga

English edition | by Cristina Berna and Eric Thomsen

No reviews

Paperback

€21.55 €21.55

Get it **Tuesday, 2 May** - **Wednesday, 24 May**

€5.59 delivery

Hokusai 53 Stations of the Tōkaidō 1801: Original

English edition | by Cristina Berna and Eric Thomsen

3.0*3.0 out of 5 stars* (1)

Paperback

€116.94 €116.94

Get it **Wednesday, 26 Apr - Friday, 19 May**

€5.68 delivery

Only 3 left in stock.

Hokusai 53 Stations of the Tōkaidō 1802: Premium

English edition | by Cristina Berna and Eric Thomsen

No reviews

Hardcover

€25.33 €25.33

Get it **Wednesday, 26 Apr** - **Friday, 19 May**

€5.79 delivery

Only 3 left in stock.

Hiroshige Famous Places of Naniwa (Osaka): Premium

English edition | by Cristina Berna and Eric Thomsen

5.0*5.0 out of 5 stars* (1)

Hardcover

€43.10 €43.10

Get it **Wednesday, 26 Apr** - **Friday, 19 May**

€5.75 delivery

Only 3 left in stock.

Christkindl Markt Wien

by Cristina Berna and Eric Thomsen

1.0*1.0 out of 5 stars* (1)

Paperback

€22.62 €22.62

Get it **Tuesday, 2 May** - **Wednesday, 24 May**

€5.59 delivery

Missy's Clan - The Beginning

English edition | by Cristina Berna and Eric Thomsen

No reviews

Paperback

€16.19 €16.19

Get it **Tuesday, 2 May** - **Wednesday, 24 May**

€5.55 delivery

Missy's Clan - Deer Friends

English edition | by Cristina Berna and Eric Thomsen

No reviews

Paperback

€16.27 €16.27

Get it **Tuesday, 2 May** - **Wednesday, 24 May**

€5.55 delivery

Missy's Clan - Models

English edition | by Cristina Berna and Eric Thomsen

No reviews

Paperback

€16.70 €16.70

Get it **Tuesday, 2 May** - **Wednesday, 24 May**

€5.55 delivery

Hiroshige 53 Stations of the Tōkaidō Jinbutso

English edition | by Cristina Berna and Eric Thomsen

2.0*2.0 out of 5 stars* (5)

Paperback

€32.80 €32.80

Get it **Tuesday, 2 May** - **Wednesday, 24 May**

€5.76 delivery

DO YOU NEED HELP?

Visit the help section or contact us

Let us look closer at these offers, because all these books appear to be “cancelled” by Ingram abt two years ago, and you wonder, how can they sell them all, then?

Especially, as authors we wonder how they can sell all these books without giving us, the copyright holders, sales reports and pay us accrued author´s fees?

Just to dispel any notion that we the authors of these books have failed to inform Amazon or Ingram of copyright, here is again the standard copyright statement which is typically found on page 2 in every one of our books, above the ISBN number.....

First, Missy´s Clan Edication:

Missy's Clan
Education
Cristina Berna
Eric Thomsen

Missy's Clan - Education Paperback – Illustrated, 18 Feb. 2019

English edition by Cristina Berna (Autor), Eric Thomsen (Autor)

No reviews

See all formats and editions

- **Paperback**
  €16.23
  Other new from €15.78

Product details

- **Publisher** : Missys Clan; Illustrated edition (18 Feb. 2019)
- **Language** : English
- **Paperback** : 42 pages
- **ISBN-10** : 2919787543
- **ISBN-13** : 978-2919787548
- **Dimensions** : 15.24 x 0.23 x 22.86 cm

This book is one of our true cat stories based on the clan of kittens by Missy, a young stray kitten that befriended Cristina.

The ISBN number is from the National ISBN Number Provider in Luxembourg.

The volume was first published 18 Feb 2019, when we were living in Salzburg.

The offer from Amazon is:

- **Paperback**
  €16.23
  Other new from €15.78

Click on the "purchases" rectangle and you get no response.

Click on "other new" – you get an offer from Amazon UK in a drop-down:

Missy's Clan - Education
Paperback

New
€6.98€6.98

FREE Shipping

Submit Add to Basket

Dispatches from

Amazon UK

Sold by

Amazon UK Return policy

Note

- International products are sold from abroad and may differ from local products, including fit, age rating, and language of product, labelling or instructions. ... More

See less

Then you get two more offers – one from Amazon US with a warning they can´t ship to "your destination" (Austria) and the other one is from Bigly Books in Scotland.

New

€7.82 €7.82

Shipping (currently unavailable)

This item cannot be shipped to your selected delivery location. Please choose a different delivery location.

Submit Add to Basket

Dispatches from

Amazon US

Sold by

Amazon US Return policy

Note

- International products are sold from abroad and may differ from local products, including fit, age rating, and language of product, labelling or instructions. ... More

---

New

€16.23 €16.23

€5.54 delivery **May 2 - 24**. Details

Submit Add to Basket

Dispatches from

Bigly Books.

Sold by

Bigly Books.

(25 ratings)
89% positive over last 12 months

Return policy

You note that Amazon UK is offering a NEW book for €6.98 and with free shipping.

How is that possible?

This is far below list price and cost price.

This is without any author´s fees…

Amazon US is offering the same book for €7.82. It says

New
€7.82 €7.82

(enhanced size, yellow coloring added)

This means the Amazon organization possesses at least two brand new copies of a book that was "cancelled" abt two years ago – is Jeff Bezos really trying to convince us that he bought a stack of these books and had them sitting for two years or more in one of his big warehouses, just waiting for this day (7 Apr 2023) to be able to offer them at a huge DISCOUNT to what he paid for them originally??

Bigly Books is also into the supply game with an offer for

New
€16.23 €16.23

(size enhanced, yellow color added)

But Bigly wants to earn a bit more – the price is €16.23 and €5.54 delivery.

This is still below list price.

This is an interesting business model that explains the success of Amazon and its network of "trusted sellers " – you buy a lot of books at full list price, then you store them for two or more years and then you offer them for sale as "New"... at a huge discount.

That is how you become the richest man, almost – in the world!

Let us look at the next offer from the Bigly storefront at Amazon.com:

Christmas
Market
Malaga
Cristina Berna
Eric Thomsen

Christmas Market Malaga Paperback – Illustrated, 6 Dec. 2019

English edition by Cristina Berna (Autor), Eric Thomsen (Autor)

No reviews

See all formats and editions

- **Paperback**
  €21.55
  Other new from €20.96

Product details

- **Publisher** : Missys Clan; Illustrated edition (6 Dec. 2019)
- **Language** : English
- **Paperback** : 100 pages
- **ISBN-10** : 2919787373
- **ISBN-13** : 978-2919787371
- **Dimensions** : 15.24 x 0.53 x 22.86 cm

It is again one of the ISBN numbers we got from the Luxembourg authority.

The book was first published 6 Dec 2019 and it was "cancelled" by Ingram abt two years ago.

So, how does Amazon get this book – as NEW??

We click on the link

Other new from €20.96

You see – it says "New"....

The drop-down shows Amazon US as seller, but warns they can´t ship to Europe:

Christmas Market Malaga
Paperback

New
€9.00 €9.00

Shipping (currently unavailable)

This item cannot be shipped to your selected delivery location. Please choose a different delivery location.

Submit Add to Basket

Dispatches from

Amazon US

Sold by

Amazon US Return policy

Note

- International products are sold from abroad and may differ from local products, including fit, age rating, and language of product, labelling or instructions. ... More

See less

Amazon US is charging €9.00 for this book, well below what they paid for it more than two years ago – if they paid.....

There are two other seller options:

New

€13.59 €13.59

FREE Shipping

Submit Add to Basket

Dispatches from

Amazon UK

Sold by

Amazon UK Return policy

Note

- International products are sold from abroad and may differ from local products, including fit, age rating, and language of product, labelling or instructions. ... More

New

€21.55 €21.55

€5.59 delivery **May 2 - 24**. Details

Submit Add to Basket

Dispatches from

Bigly Books.

Sold by

Bigly Books.

(25 ratings)
89% positive over last 12 months

Return policy

End of results

Amazon UK is also offering the book at a loss - €13.59 – and Bigly Books tries to recover a bit more….€21.55.

You marvel at the Amazon "get rich quick" business model – buy expensive, store for more than two years – and sell at a huge loss!!

This is why Elon Musk is the richest man in the World and not Jeff Bezos…..

If you click the link

See all formats and editions

You get this offer from Amazon in a drop-down:

1 formats and editions How are results ordered?

- **Paperback, Illustrated (1)**

Christmas Market Malaga

€9.00 €9.00

New from €9.00

Rating	(0)
ISBN-13	978-2919787371
Publisher	Missys Clan
Edition	Illustrated
Publication Date	6 Dec. 2019

The question is trivial – how can Amazon offer this title for sale as "New" when the title has been "cancelled" by Ingram more abt two years ago?

What kind of deal is there between Ingram and Amazon?

Bigly Books also do not report any sales data and do not pay any author´s fees.

None of them reports any sales to the authors and none of them pays any author´s fees.

Let us continue to the third offer

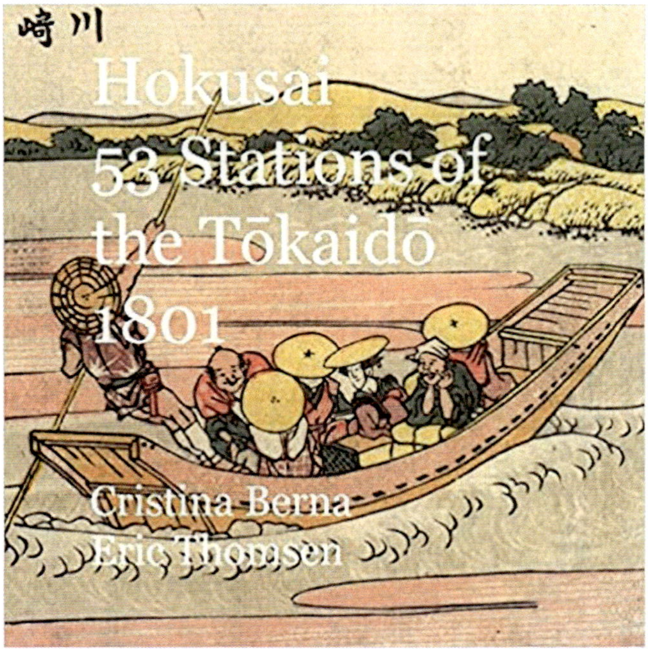

Hokusai 53 Stations of the Tōkaidō 1801: Original Paperback – 16 Sept. 2020

English edition by Cristina Berna (Autor), Eric Thomsen (Autor)

3.0 out of 5 stars 1 rating

See all formats and editions

- Hardcover
  —

- **Paperback**
  €116.94
  Other new from €113.75

This version of Hokusai 53 Stations of the Tokaido is stitched together as the original series in 1801 – when you open the pages, the two prints are on the opposing pages, and then our text, which was not in the original series, is in the next double spread, thereby giving you an "original" like experience when you page through the book.

Note again the offer is for "New" -

Other new from €113.75

(enhanced type, yellow added).

The drop-down shows Amazon UK as the first seller:

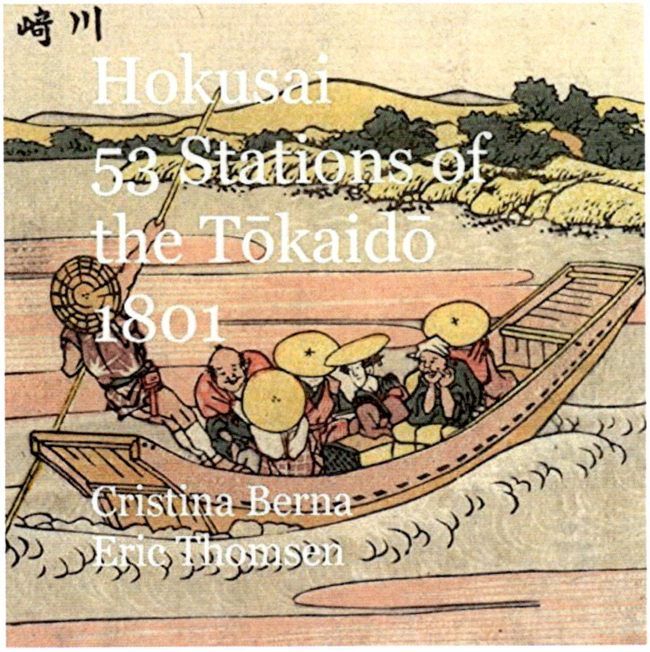

Hokusai 53 Stations of the Tōkaidō 1801: Original
Paperback

1 rating

New
€95.02 €95.02

FREE Shipping

Submit Add to Basket

Dispatches from

Amazon UK

Sold by

Amazon UK Return policy

Note

- International products are sold from abroad and may differ from local products, including fit, age rating, and language of product, labelling or instructions. ... More

See less

Amazon UK charges €95,02 for this new book.

Now, there are three more sellers:

New

€113.47 €113.47

€5.68 delivery **May 24 - June 2**. Details

Submit Add to Basket

Dispatches from

~~V KING~~

Sold by

~~V KING~~

(33 ratings)
67% positive over last 12 months

Return policy

New

€116.94 €116.94

€5.68 delivery **April 26 - May 19**. Details

Submit Add to Basket

Dispatches from

Bigly Books.

Sold by

Bigly Books.

(25 ratings)
89% positive over last 12 months

Return policy

New

€117.43 €117.43

€5.68 delivery **May 22 - 31**. Details

Submit Add to Basket

Dispatches from

BOOKSXPRESS USA

Sold by

BOOKSXPRESS USA

(1201 ratings)
71% positive over last 12 months

Return policy

End of results

V-king is offering a

New book at
€113.47 €113.47

Our search partner Bigly Books is offering

New book at
€95.02 €95.02

And

Booksexpress USA is offering

New

€117.43 €117.43

This means there exists at least FOUR (4) new copies of this book (7 Apr 2023) now abt two years after Ingram "cancelled" the title and officially stopped printing it – print on demand – print a single volume at a time against cash – no bulk orders!

Who are these people who stock books for many years and then sell them at a discount to what they originally paid?

What is the business model?

Are they "money laundering" illicit drug cash this way?

It is cheaper to buy Danish State lotto for that purpose! Or go to the casino!

Click on the link

~~V KING~~

and you get the following "trusted seller" information:

Detailed Seller Information
Business seller

Business Name: V-King Services

Business Type: Privately-owned business

Trade Register Number: 881884373

VAT Number: DE341157560

Business Address:

1001

Route du Port

Hinx

40180

FR

There is a "storefront" ... Visit the ~~V KING~~ storefront

If you click this store you get 100,000 books that V-King offers, displayed 16 per page, and if you search V-King store for the author "Cristina Berna", you get...

No results for Cristina Berna.

Price and other details may vary based on product size and colour.
cristinaSee all 7 results

If you click the link
BOOKSXPRESS USA

You get the following Amazon "trusted seller" information

Detailed Seller Information
Business seller

Business Name: BOOKSXPRESS EU LLC

Business Type: Privately-owned business

Trade Register Number: 83-3670642

VAT Number: GB320495520

Phone number: +1 347-692-8950

Business Address:

295 Concord Dr

FREEHOLD

NJ

07728-4229

US

There is again a “storefront” inside Amazon with

1-16 of over 100,000 results

Sort by: Featured Sort by:Featured

RESULTS

Learn about these results.

Wie der Westen den Krieg in die Ukraine Brachte: Die Rolle der USA und der NATO im Ukraine-Konflikt

by Benjamin Abelow

4.3*4.3 out of 5 stars* (69)

Paperback

€15.68 €15.68

Get it **Thursday, 11 May - Monday, 22 May**

€5.58 delivery

You can´t copy paste “BOOKEXPRESS” from the search bar where “all departments” is usually displayed in the amazon website, but we have a photo…

The result is

No results for Cristina Berna.

Price and other details may vary based on product size and colour.
Cristina See all 6 results

Let us now continue our journey with Amazon to the third book of the 16.

This is our book Hokusai 53 Stations of the Tokaido 1802 series in the premium version we sold via Ingram until they abruptly without good cause “cancelled” this book abt two years ago.

Hokusai had done the 1801 series see above and the publishers sold them quickly and asked for a new series for 1802, and this is the one.

We tried on Ingram to offer our books in paperback, the cheapest and poorest quality, hardback in the middle and premium with the best quality paper and color that Ingram offered, and at a higher price so customers had a price and quality choice.

Click on the title and you get:

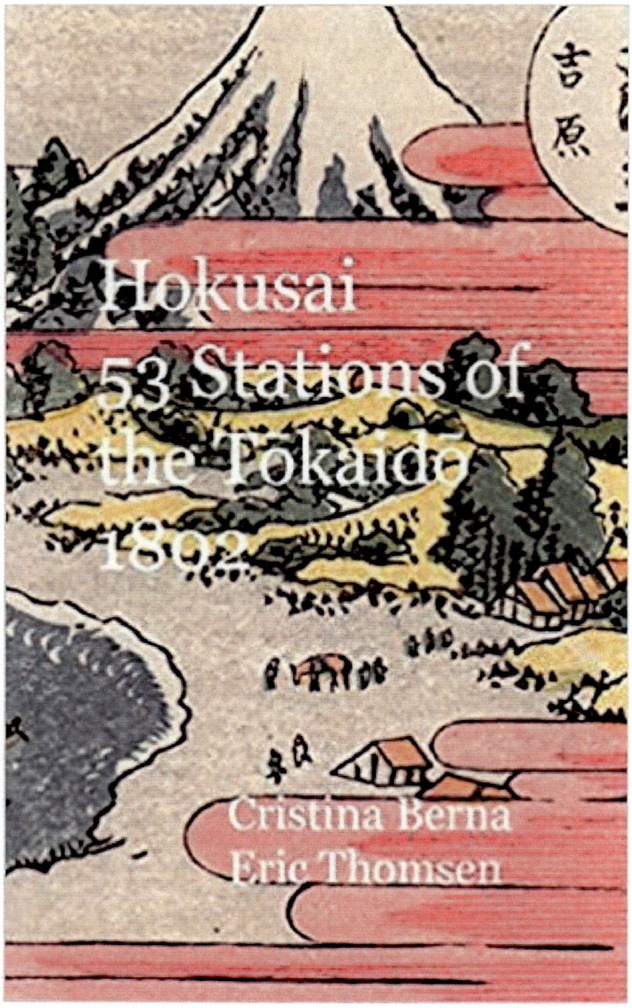

Hokusai 53 Stations of the Tōkaidō 1802:

Premium **Hardcover – 12 Oct. 2020**

English edition by Cristina Berna (Autor), Eric Thomsen (Autor)

No reviews

See all formats and editions

- **Hardcover**
  €25.33
  Other new from €24.64

Click on the kink Other new from €24.64 and you get this offer:

Note the books are offered as "New" – how on Earth can they do that when Ingram officially stopped production after "cancelling" the books abt two years ago???

How can all the books on the Bigly Books storefront list be "New"? What kind of mega operation is Bigly that they can store all obscure writers like us??

Hokusai 53 Stations of the Tōkaidō 1802: Premium
Hardcover

New

€25.33 €25.33

€5.79 delivery **April 26 - May 19**. Details

Submit Add to Basket

Dispatches from

Bigly Books.

Sold by

Bigly Books.

(25 ratings)
89% positive over last 12 months

Return policy

See less

Look, friends – just look up Bigly Books Ltd in Companies House – link is

https://find-and-update.company-information.service.gov.uk/company/SC646707

BIGLY BOOKS LTD

Company number SC646707

Nature of business (SIC)

47910 - Retail sale via mail order houses or via Internet

Are you seriously claiming Bigly Books Ltd has these books in physical storage and are not printing them or getting them printed on demand from the pdf files that we uploaded to Ingram??

Are you seriously claiming that Bigly Books Ltd is selling a hard cover book in premium quality paper and premium quality ink for less than Ingram charged us for printing the same book?

€25.33.....

Who are you kidding?

Now look at the four other offers:

New

€27.09 €27.09

€5.79 delivery **May 19 - 30**. Details

Submit Add to Basket

Dispatches from

BOOKSXPRESS USA

Sold by

BOOKSXPRESS USA

(1201 ratings)
71% positive over last 12 months

Return policy

New

€26.35€ 26.35

€5.79 delivery **May 23 - June 1**. Details

Submit Add to Basket

Dispatches from

~~V KING~~

Sold by

~~V KING~~

(33 ratings)
67% positive over last 12 months

Return policy

New

€36.09 €36.09

FREE delivery **May 2 - 24**. Details

Submit Add to Basket

Dispatches from

Paragon OS

Sold by

Paragon OS

(194 ratings)
88% positive over last 12 months

Return policy

New

€105.37 €105.37

FREE delivery **Friday, April 14**

Submit Add to Basket

Dispatches from

Amazon

Sold by

Amazon
Return policy

End of results

Now these online "bookstores" suddenly have our books when they didn´t have any on the author specific search....

BOOKSEXPRESS the link is
BOOKSXPRESS USA

Is offering

New
€27.09 €27.09

But, wait a minute.....we saw above the Booksesexpress USA don´t offer any books by Cristina Berna, so what is this they are doing? It just "pop up"??

And a "New" book which has been out of print for abt two years???

The same about V King the link is
~~V KING~~

And they offer

New
€26.35 €26.35

And now you also have a seller Paragon?

Paragon the link is

Paragon OS

Offering

New

€36.09

We also see that Amazon itself is offering

New

€105.37 €105.37

We have at least five (5) brand new copies in various places of the world of a book which was “cancelled” and out of print for abt two years.

We can go back to our sales statistics from Ingram and we would use that to dispute that these books have existed in the period between “cancellation” and the search (7 Apr 2023) - we suspect that these books are or will be printed from the pdf files we uploaded to Ingram 12 Oct 2020 and somehow Amazon is able to activate these files and print more copies without giving us sales statistics and without Amazon paying us author´s fees?

If you click the link See all formats and editions

You get the following information in the form of a drop-down with no link displayed

1 formats and editions How are results ordered?

- **Hardcover**
  (1)

Hokusai 53 Stations of the Tōkaidō 1802: Premium

€25.33 €25.33
New from €24.64

Rating	(0)
ISBN-13	978-1649454690
Publisher	Missys Clan
Publication Date	12 Oct. 2020

Go now to the fifth book offered in the search on Bigly Books Ltd:

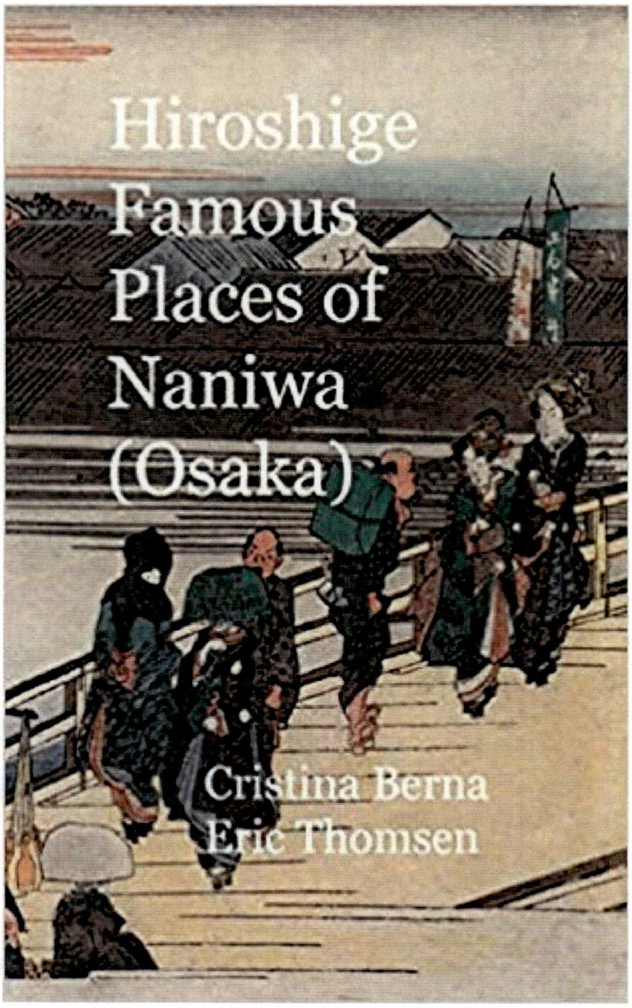

Product details

- **Publisher** : Missys Clan (16 Nov. 2020)
  Language : English

- **Hardcover** : 154 pages
- **ISBN-10** : 1649454511
- **ISBN-13** : 978-1649454515
- **Dimensions** : 15.19 x 1.42 x 22.91 cm
-
- **Customer reviews:**
  *5.0 out of 5 stars_* 1 rating

Hiroshige Famous Places of Naniwa (Osaka): Premium Hardcover – 16 Nov. 2020

English edition by Cristina Berna (Autor), Eric Thomsen (Autor)

*5.0 out of 5 stars_* 1 rating

See all formats and editions

- **Hardcover**
  €43.10
  Other new from €41.92

- Paperback
  €33.19
  Other new from €32.28

'

This book has an ISBN number we purchased from ISBN Services Inch in New York – we have an invoice….

It was published via Ingram 16 Nov 2020 and "cancelled" by Ingram for no good reason abt two years ago, meaning if the sellers didn´t buy it before that, they can´t lawfully buy this book from ??? and sell it – it will be a counterfeit or fraud.

There is a link to hardcover

Other new from €41.92

Click on that and you get the following offers:

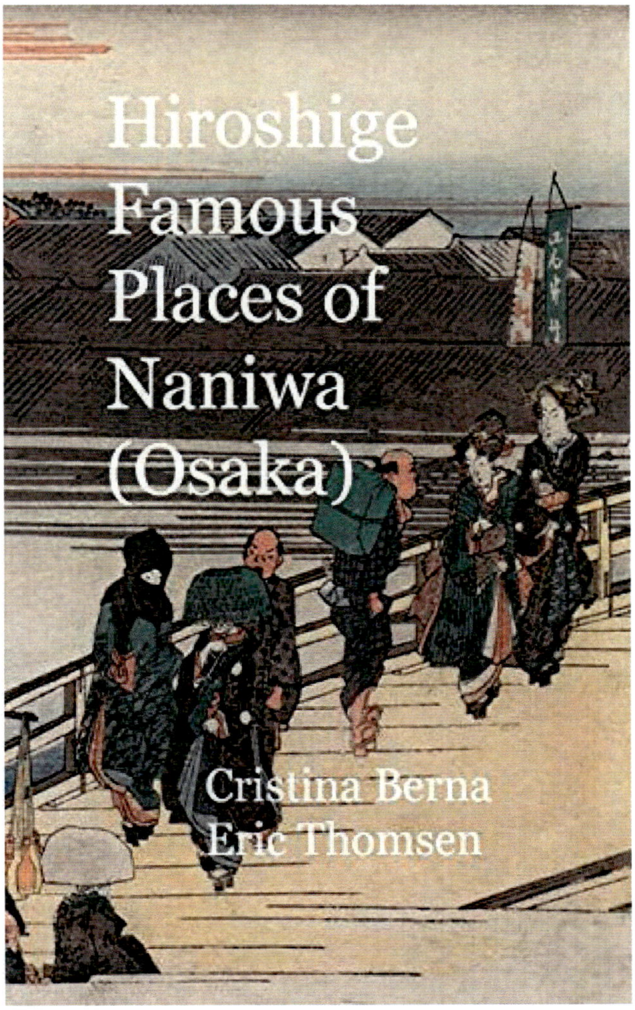

Hiroshige Famous Places of Naniwa (Osaka): Premium
Hardcover

1 rating

New

€43.10 €43.10

€5.75 delivery **April 26 - May 19**. Details

Submit Add to Basket

Dispatches from

Bigly Books.

Sold by

Bigly Books.

(25 ratings)
89% positive over last 12 months

Return policy

See less

Our friend Bigly Books Ltd is offering

New

€43.10 €43.10

Where has he got this book from? It has been "cancelled" for abt two years – you can´t buy this book from the rightful owner´s representative at that time – Ingram – as far as we know.

We don’t get any sales statistics and Ingram also does not send us any author´s fees and Bigly also gives no statistics or pay any fees itself.

So much for the review that our books are expensive see later – we are not getting paid for a fraction of the number of books that appears to be sold....

There is one more offer:

New

€102.16 €102.16

FREE delivery **Thursday, April 13**

Submit Add to Basket

Dispatches from

Amazon

Sold by

Amazon
Return policy

End of results

This is Amazon in London...they offer

New
€102.16 €102.16

Where does Amazon get this book from?

We see there exists at least two (2) brand new copies of this book in the UK.

Click now on "paperback"...

You get this information

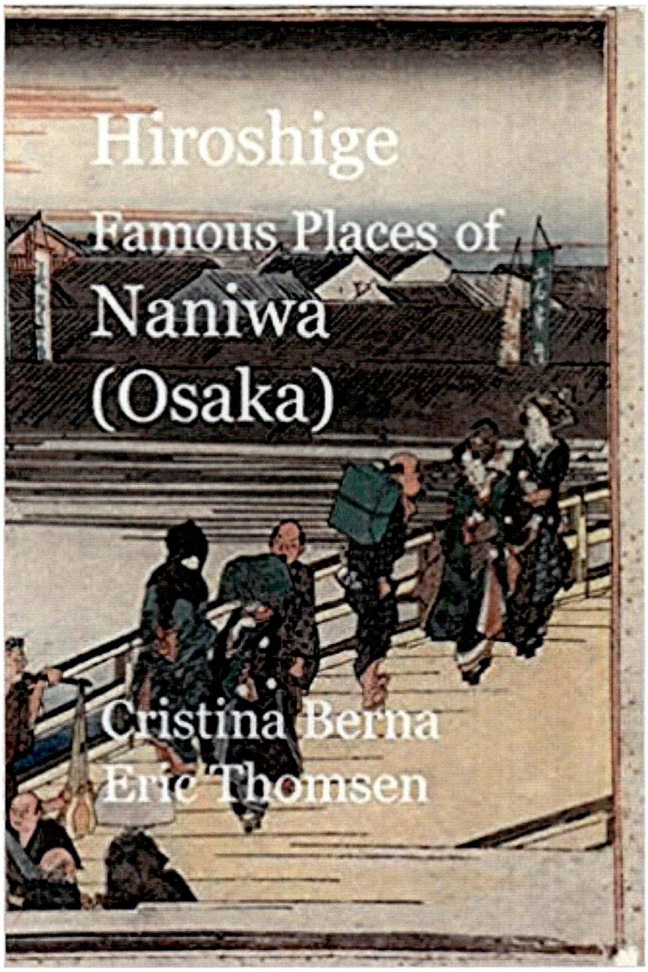

Hiroshige Famous Places of Naniwa

(Osaka) Paperback – 9 Jun. 2020

English edition by Cristina Berna (Autor), Eric Thomsen (Autor)

5.0 out of 5 stars 1 rating

See all formats and editions

- Hardcover
  €43.10
  Other new from €41.92

- **Paperback**
  €41.93
  Other new from €32.28

Product details

- **Publisher** : Missys Clan (9 Jun. 2020)
- **Language** : English
- **Paperback** : 152 pages
- **ISBN-10** : 1649454996
- **ISBN-13** : 978-1649454997
- **Dimensions** : 15.24 x 0.84 x 22.86 cm
- **Customer reviews:**

  5.0 out of 5 stars 1 rating r

We have a five-star rating for this book. Thank you, unknown customer!

We didn´t pay anybody to give us five stars, someone was obviously happy with our work and decided to commend it. Presumably they paid for it, but were we paid?

Now, click on the link

- Other new from €32.28

And you get these offers:

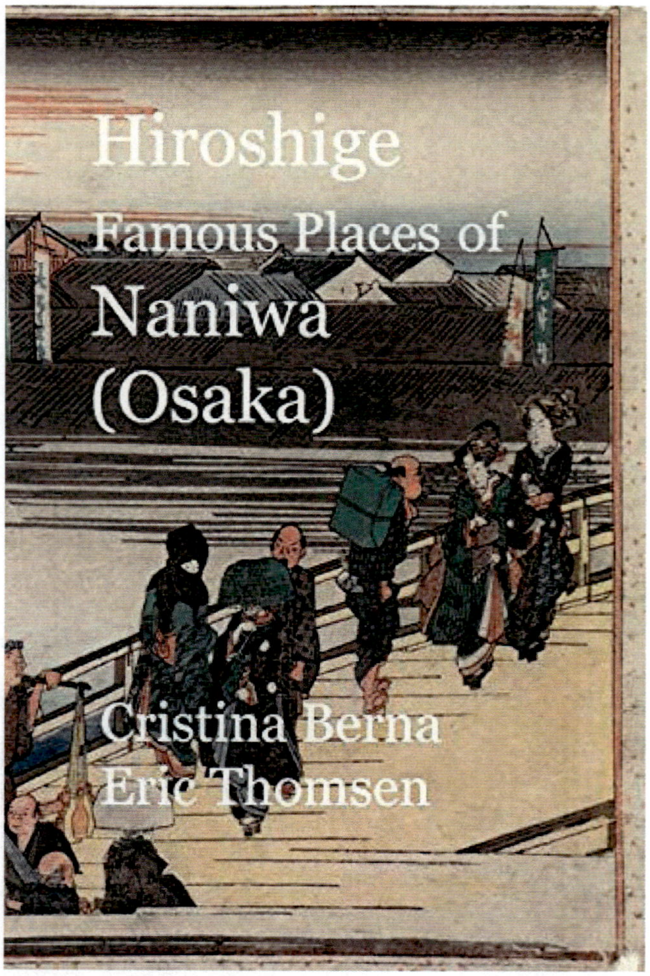

Hiroshige Famous Places of Naniwa (Osaka)
Paperback

1 rating

New
€41.93 €41.93

FREE delivery **Tuesday, April 11**. Order within 8 hrs 24 mins

Submit Add to Basket

Dispatches from

Amazon

Sold by

Amazon
Return policy

See less

And our friend Bigly Books Ltd with

New
€33.19

€5.63 delivery **May 2 - 24**. Details

Submit Add to Basket

Dispatches from

Bigly Books.

Sold by

Bigly Books.

(25 ratings)
89% positive over last 12 months

Return policy

Amazon UK is offering

New
€41.93 €41.93

and

Biggly is offering

New
€3319 €33.19

Now, remember the ISBN number - 978-1649454997 – it is one we bought from ISBN Services Inc in New York – we have the invoice and we paid for it....

If you go now to the new platform we have found where we re-issue the books "cancelled" by Ingram, we offer

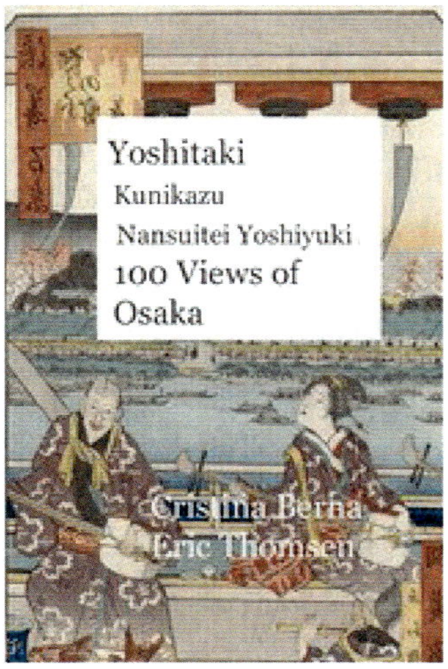

Yoshitaki Kunikazu Nansuitei Yoshiyuki 100 Views of Osaka

Cristina Berna Precio 99.95€ ISBN 9781956773965

We will come to this book later as it is one of the first 16 we have uploaded with our agent .....

But you see that Amazon and Bigly Books Ltd are dumping the price of our legal version which cost €99.95 for the paperback, where they charge €41.93 and e33.19 respectively.

And Amazon does NOT link to the legal version, they link to the counterfeit versions which they dump as they able to do for one thing because they don´t pay any author´s fees.

This appears to be willful and malicious copyright infringement.

Of course the customer will want to buy the cheaper versions, if Amazon is also printing in the same poor quality the legal version we have uploaded via our agent.

Amazon and Bigly are also not telling the customers that their offered versions are counterfeit. Our books surely still have the copyright notice inside – Amazon and Bigly has not added a stamp saying "counterfeit"….???

No, they claim they are "New".

How can they sell as "New" books that they have had in storage for more than two years, if that is what they will claim??

No, we believe Amazon and Bigly are printing from the pdf files we uploaded to Ingram and where Ingram "cancelled" these books for no good reason – as Amazon and Bigly are happy to sell them!

We have a long email correspondence with Ingram but nowhere has Ingram informed us they have turned over our copyrighted pdf files to Amazon or any third party for use without paying author´s fees – and we would of course never have accepted that! We want to earn some income from our hard labor.

But we are not done yet – Bigly Books Ltd also offers:

Christkindl Markt Wien Paperback – Illustrated, 25 Jan. 2019

by Cristina Berna (Autor), Eric Thomsen (Autor)

1.0 out of 5 stars 1 rating

See all formats and editions

- Hardcover
  —

- **Paperback**
  €22.62
  Other new from €22.00

·

Product details

- **Publisher :** Missys Clan; Illustrated edition (25 Jan. 2019)
- **Language :** German
- **Paperback :** 94 pages
- **ISBN-10 :** 2919787063
- **ISBN-13 :** 978-2919787067
- **Dimensions :** 15.24 x 0.48 x 22.86 cm
- **Best Sellers Rank:** 3,378,884 in Books (See Top 100 in Books)
  - 3,961 in Travel Photography (Books)
  - 11,078 in Entrepreneurship (Books)

    - 22,041 in Business Development & Entrepreneurship (Books)
- **Customer reviews:**
  *1.0 out of 5 stars_* 1 rating

This book only has one star – it has great pictures, they are our own from a visit to this Christmas Market, they are not from the internet. The sky had a fantastic blue and people were happy. It was before the China Virus

Click on the link Other new from €22.00 and you get this offer:

Christkindl Markt Wien
Paperback

1 rating

New
€22.62 €22.62

€5.59 delivery **May 2 - 24**. Details

Submit Add to Basket

Dispatches from

Bigly Books.

Sold by

Bigly Books.

(25 ratings)
89% positive over last 12 months

Return policy

See less

Now, there is another link See all formats and editions

Which gives you this resut:

- Hardcover, Illustrated (1)
- **Paperback, Illustrated (1)**

Christkindl Markt Wien

€22.62 €22.62

New from €22.00

Rating	(1)
ISBN-13	978-2919787067
Publisher	Missys Clan
Edition	Illustrated
Publication Date	25 Jan. 2019

The paperback, and the hardcover version:

2 formats and editions How are results ordered?

- **Hardcover, Illustrated (1)**
- Paperback, Illustrated (1)

Christkindl Markt Wien

€42.42 €42.42

Rating	(0)
ISBN-13	978-2919787128
Publisher	Missys Clan
Edition	Illustrated
Publication Date	11 Feb. 2019

Again the trivial question – where do they get these books?

Ingram "cancelled" them - all 291 titles - abt two years ago and has not sent sales statistics or author´s fees – and Bigly also is not sending sales statistics and author´s fees.

The seventh book on the search result for Bigly Books, for author Cristina Berna, is

Missy's Clan
The Beginning
Cristina Berna
Eric Thomsen

Missy's Clan - The Beginning Paperback – Illustrated, 25 Feb. 2019

English edition by Cristina Berna (Autor), Eric Thomsen (Autor)

No reviews

See all formats and editions

- **Paperback**
  €16.19
  Other new from €15.75

Product details

- **Publisher** : Missys Clan; Illustrated edition (25 Feb. 2019)
- **Language** : English
- **Paperback** : 46 pages
- **ISBN-10** : 2919787969
- **ISBN-13** : 978-2919787968
- **Dimensions** : 15.24 x 0.25 x 22.86 cm

In this book we tell you how Missy´s Clan all started.

It is a charming little true cat story which Ingram “cancelled” for no good reason abt two years ago. The ISBN number is one of the 200 we got while we were living in Luxembourg and enjoyed good cake.

Click on the link Other new from €15.75 and you get these offers:

Amazon UK

Missy's Clan - The Beginning
Paperback

New
€6.98 €6.98

FREE Shipping

Submit Add to Basket

Dispatches from

Amazon UK

Sold by

Amazon UK Return policy

Note

- International products are sold from abroad and may differ from local products, including fit, age rating, and language of product, labelling or instructions. ... More

See less

And Bigly Books Ltd

New

€16.19 €16.19

€5.55 delivery **May 2 - 24**. Details

Submit Add to Basket

Dispatches from

Bigly Books.

Sold by

Bigly Books.

(25 ratings)
89% positive over last 12 months

Return policy

End of results

You see Amazon offers

New
€6.98

And Bigly offers

New
€16.19

How to they get our books as “New” when they have not been lawfully printed for abt two years when Ingram “cancelled” all our 291 titles for no good reason?

Do they have access to the pdf files we uploaded to Ingram???

How can that be????

Click also on the link See all formats and editions and you see

1 formats and editions How are results ordered?

- **Paperback, Illustrated (1)**

Missy's Clan - The Beginning

€6.98 €6.98

New from €6.98

Rating	(0)
ISBN-13	978-2919787968
Publisher	Missys Clan
Edition	Illustrated
Publication Date	25 Feb. 2019

Look, we want to sell books!

We love to write books!

We love to sell books!

We write books to make an income.

Go now to the eight of our books offered by Bigly Books Ltd:

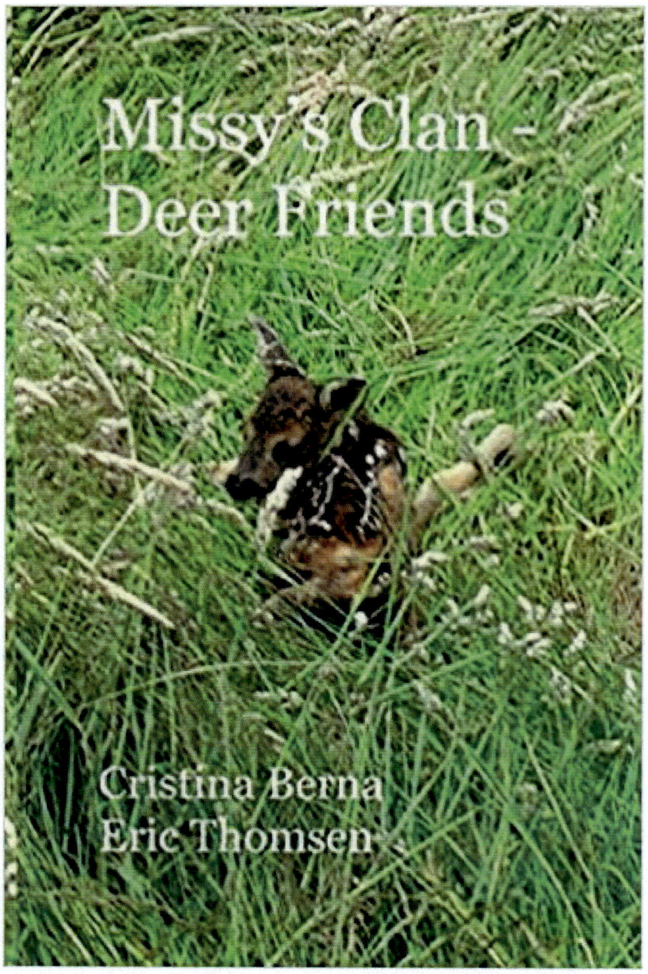
Missy's Clan -
Deer Friends
Cristina Berna
Eric Thomsen

Missy's Clan - Deer Friends Paperback – Illustrated, 18 Feb. 2019

English edition by Cristina Berna (Autor), Eric Thomsen (Autor)

No reviews

See all formats and editions

- **Paperback**
  €16.27
  Other new from €15.83

Product details

- **Publisher** : Missys Clan; Illustrated edition (18 Feb. 2019)
- **Language** : English
- **Paperback** : 48 pages
- **ISBN-10** : 2919787934
- **ISBN-13** : 978-2919787937
- **Dimensions** : 15.24 x 0.25 x 22.86 cm
-

Here we tell you about some fantastic encounters with wild animals – in our garden at that time.

Click on the link Other new from €15.83

and you get these offers:

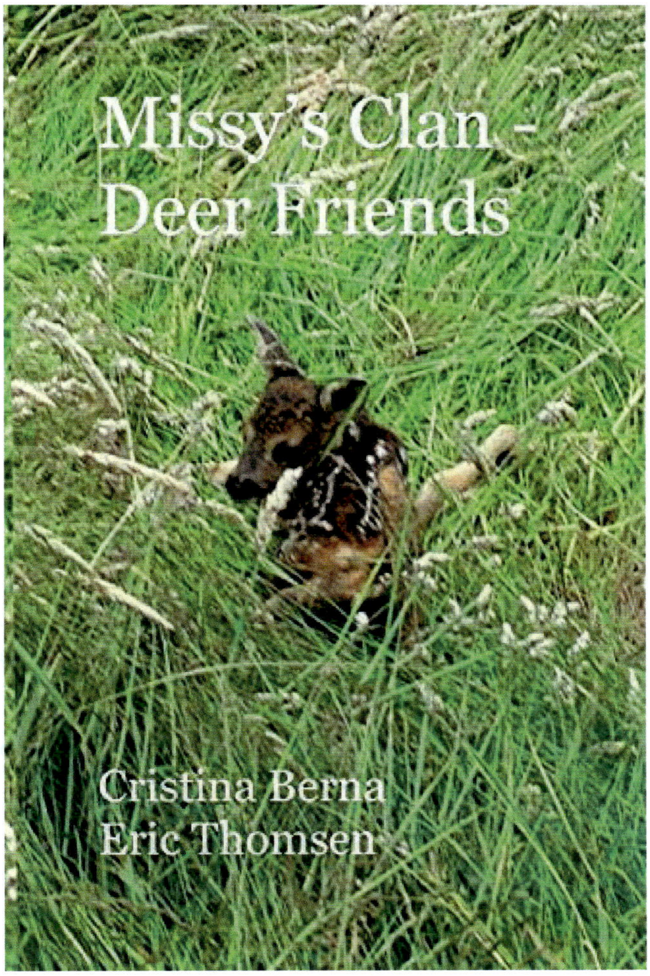

Missy's Clan - Deer Friends
Paperback

New
€16.27 €16.27

€5.55 delivery **May 2 - 24**. Details

Submit Add to Basket

Dispatches from

Bigly Books.

Sold by

Bigly Books.

(25 ratings)
89% positive over last 12 months

Return policy

See less

Currently, there are no other sellers matching your location and / or item specification. Try updating the filters or your location to find additional sellers.

Filter (1)

New

Clear all

You see Bigly offers

New

€16.27 €16.27

Another of our books which Ingram has "cancelled" abt two years ago.

Go then to the ninth book of ours Bigly offers in their search results:

Missy's Clan - Models Paperback – Illustrated, 15 April 2019

English edition by Cristina Berna (Autor), Eric Thomsen (Autor)

No reviews

See all formats and editions

- **Paperback**
  €16.70
  Other new from €16.24

Product details

- **Publisher** : Missys Clan; Illustrated edition (15 April 2019)
- **Language** : English
- **Paperback** : 54 pages
- **ISBN-10** : 2919787268
- **ISBN-13** : 978-2919787265
- **Dimensions** : 15.24 x 0.28 x 22.86 cm

Click on the link Other new from €16.24
and you get this offer:

Missy's Clan - Models
Paperback

New
€20.39 €20.39

FREE delivery **Friday, April 14**

Submit Add to Basket

Dispatches from

Amazon

Sold by

Amazon
Return policy

See less

and

New
€16.70 €16.70

€5.55 delivery **May 2 - 24**. Details

Submit Add to Basket

Dispatches from

Bigly Books.

Sold by

Bigly Books.

(25 ratings)
89% positive over last 12 months

Return policy

There are at least two copies of this book in the UK and they are sold as new, even though Ingram cancelled the title abt two years ago:

New
€16.70

Now, to the 10th book on the search with Bigly Books Ltd storefront inside the Amazon.com website:

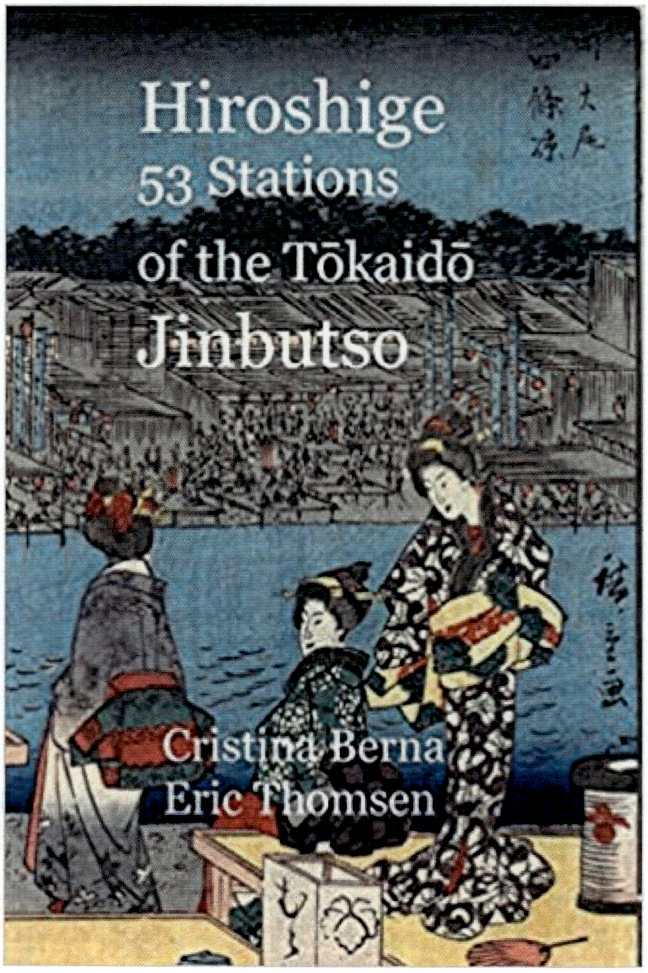

Hiroshige 53 Stations of the Tōkaidō Jinbutso

Paperback – 31 Dec. 2020

English edition by Cristina Berna (Autor), Eric Thomsen (Autor)

2.0 out of 5 stars 5 ratings

See all formats and editions

- Hardcover
  €34.18
  Other new from €33.24

- **Paperback**
  €32.80
  Other new from €31.91

Product details

- **Publisher** : Missys Clan (31 Dec. 2020)
- **Language** : English
- **Paperback** : 304 pages
- **ISBN-10** : 1637526652
- **ISBN-13** : 978-1637526651
- **Dimensions** : 15.24 x 1.63 x 22.86 cm
- **Customer reviews:**
  2.0 out of 5 stars 5 ratings

Let us first enjoy the reviews:

Top review from Germany

Amazon Kunde

1.0 out of 5 stars **A bit disappointing**

Reviewed in Germany on 22 January 2021

Verified Purchase

Small pixelated pictures and texts copied off Wikipedia. Only thing premium is the price.

Mark this review as helpful BUTTON

Helpful

Report

This must be someone in the university, because on the one hand they sneer at Wikipedia and on the other hand he should know the entries in Wikipedia are group discussions between often highly educated specialists drawing on stacks of shown references.

This means “copied of Wikipedia” is meant as an insult and is not reflective of the quality of the information as such.

Second, this buyer bought the cheapest version – whether printed by Amazon, copied by Amazon or printed by Ingram.

The reviewer obviously did no check the format before buying.

What were the expectations from the buyer?

We don´t know, but it is someone who does not want to pay too much…..like Bigly Books and Amazon. They don´t pay the authors, regardless of what price they charge the customer. They rake it all in for themselves.

Of course the reviewer can´t know all this and it is distressing every time to have a negative review as it is important for us.

Jonyguitar

1.0 out of 5 stars **Arnaque**

Reviewed in France on 24 November 2020

Verified Purchase

Ce produit vendu au tarif exorbitant de 85 euros est une véritable arnaque :
- dimensions ridicules,
- qualité d'impression déplorable,
- images ridiculement petites.
- texte verbeux

Ne l'achetez pas c'est de l'argent gaspillé
Je l'ai renvoyé au bout de 5 minutes ...

One person found this helpful

Report

Translation by Amazon:

Jonyguitar

1.0 out of 5 stars **Scam**

Reviewed in France on 24 November 2020

Verified Purchase

This product sold at an exorbitant price of 85 euros is a real scam:

- ridiculous dimensions,
- deplorable print quality,
- ridiculously small images.
- verbose text
Don't buy it's wasted money
I sent it back after 5 minutes...

One person found this helpful

Report

Translated from French by Amazon

See original · Report translation

Oh, scam is it, Johnny??

You didn´t check the dimensions of the book before ordering it – you were looking for another type of book.

You complain about the print quality, but you bought the cheapest possible version – are your expectations really reasonable?

Ridiculous small images – so, Johnny, you were buying without considering the size of the book – how big images can you have in a small format book?

But we are sorry that you were disappointed.

You also complain about the text – "verbose" – meaning this is an extra insult.

MG

4.0 out of 5 stars **Love the information in the book**

Reviewed in the United States on 3 February 2022

Verified Purchase

I enjoyed reading the information they have researched for their book. However, I would have liked very much to see higher quality pictures for their illustrations. Also, I would have liked to have proof read their text before publication as it is obvious that English is not the writer's first or best language.

Report

We are happier about this review – four out of five stars.

Thank you for acknowledging the hard work to gather all the information.

Again, print quality corresponds to price. This book was also offered in higher quality paper and color precisely to allow upgrading for what purpose the reader had.

The reviewer correctly points out the hard work of proof reading and that even if you proof umpteen times you may still find some mistakes.

The reviewer also comments on language – that is a presumption and it would be easy to refute it, but no need to get into an argument with four stars out of five!

Thank you again!

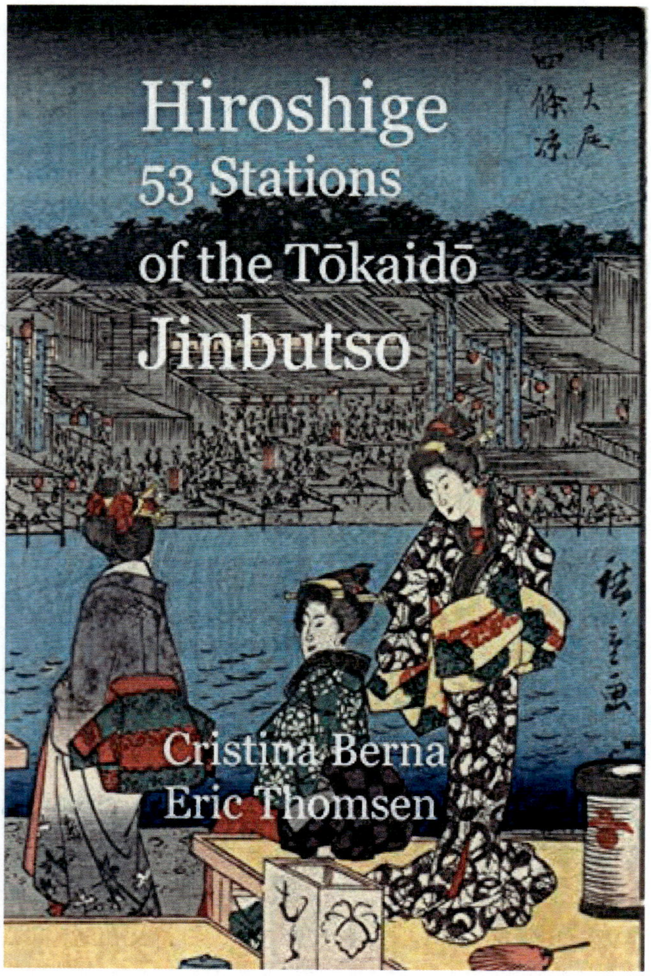

Hiroshige 53 Stations of the Tōkaidō Jinbutso
Paperback

5 ratings

New
€36.98 €36.98

FREE delivery **April 27 - May 22**. Details

Submit Add to Basket

Dispatches from

Paragon OS

Sold by

Paragon OS

(195 ratings)
88% positive over last 12 months

Return policy

See less

New

€32.80 €32.80

€5.76 delivery **May 2 - 24**. Details

Submit Add to Basket

Dispatches from

Bigly Books.

Sold by

Bigly Books.

(25 ratings)
89% positive over last 12 months

Return policy

New

€87.02 €87.02

FREE delivery **Tuesday, April 11**. Order within 8 hrs

Submit Add to Basket

Dispatches from

Amazon

Sold by

Amazon

Return policy

Paragon is offering Jinbutso at

New

€36.98 €36.98

Bigly is offering Jinbutso

New

€32.80 €32.80

Amazon UK is offering Jinbutso as

New

€87.02 €87.02

There exist at least three (3) brand new copies of this book – two in Britain and one in the US.

Paragon details:

Detailed Seller Information
Business seller

Business Name: PARAGON OS, INC.

Business Type: Privately-owned business

Trade Register Number: 47-5543814

Customer Services Address:

13401 Sutton Park Drive S.

Apt 933

JACKSONVILLE

Florida

32224

US

Business Address:

13401 SUTTON PARK DR S APT 933

APT 933

Jacksonville

FL

32224-5283

US

Look him up on google maps – no big warehouse there! But he can have the warehouse in China, of course.

But Jinbutso is also available in higher quality - only there is an error in the Amazon machine here.

If you click on hardcover, you get a drop down, but with information about another completely different book, same theme, but a series Hiroshige did 20 years earlier – his first, actually:

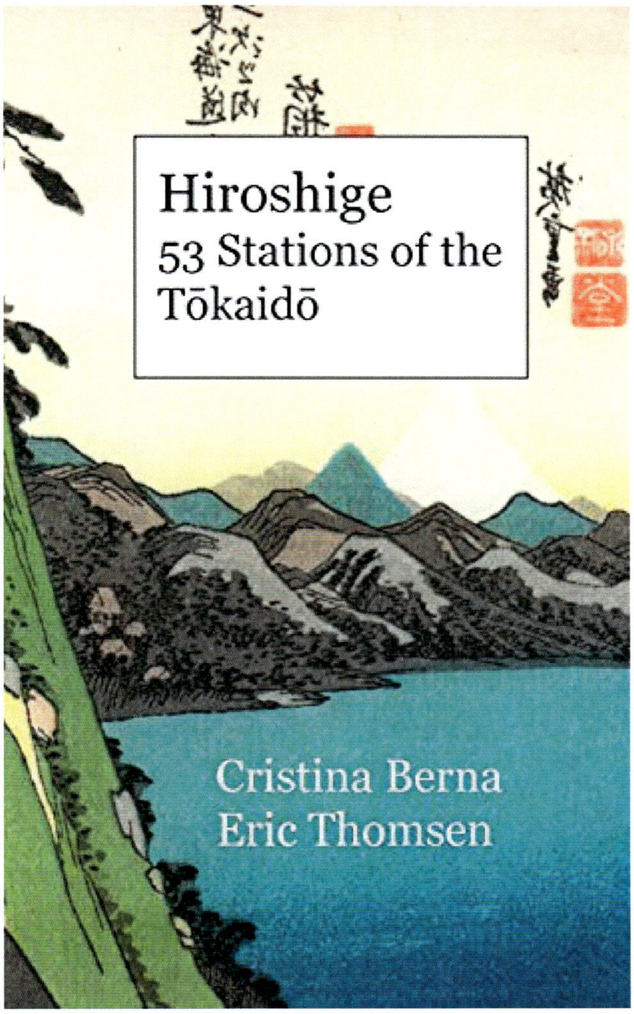

Hiroshige 53 Stations of the Tokaido: Premium
Hardcover

5 ratings

New

€34.18 €34.18

€5.84 delivery **May 2 - 24**. Details

Submit Add to Basket

Dispatches from

Bigly Books.

Sold by

Bigly Books.

(25 ratings)
89% positive over last 12 months

Return policy

New
€105.24 €105.24

FREE delivery **Wednesday, April 12**

Submit Add to Basket

Dispatches from

Amazon

Sold by

Amazon
Return policy

Also this other work is offered as hardback and NEW in spite it was "cancelled" by Ingram abt two years ago – so where do they get all these books?

Bigly

New

€34.18 €34.18

Amazon

New

€105.24 €105.24

,

Paragon is offering 17 works by the authors, but we will refrain from a detailed examination of them at this time.

Suffice to list them:

https://www.amazon.de/s?k=cristina+berna&me=A2UPJU7HJNUPBC&ref=nb_sb_noss

(search 7 Apr 2023)

RESULTS

Learn about these results.

Joaquín Sorolla Familie

by Cristina Berna

New to Amazon

[Paperback]

€173.02 €173.02

Get it **Tuesday, 2 May** - **Wednesday, 24 May**

FREE Delivery

Kuwagata Keisai (Kitao Masayoshi) Methods of Cursive Drawing of Landscapes Coloring and Pattern Book

English edition | by Cristina Berna

5.0*5.0 out of 5 stars* (1)

Paperback

€89.60 €89.60

Get it **Thursday, 27 Apr - Monday, 22 May**

FREE Delivery

Joaquín Sorolla Nudes

English edition | by Cristina Berna

1.41.4 out of 5 stars (3)

Paperback

€140.77 €140.77

Get it **Tuesday, 2 May** - **Wednesday, 24 May**

FREE Delivery

Hokusai 53 Stations of the Tōkaidō 1801 square

English edition | by Cristina Berna and Eric Thomsen

3.03.0 out of 5 stars (1)

Paperback

€31.99 €31.99

Get it **Tuesday, 2 May** - **Wednesday, 24 May**

FREE Delivery

Hokusai 53 Stations of the Tōkaidō 1804 Vertical

English edition | by Cristina Berna and Eric Thomsen

No reviews

Paperback

€31.89 €31.89

Get it **Tuesday, 2 May** - **Wednesday, 24 May**

FREE Delivery

Hokusai 53 Stations of the Tōkaidō 1804 Horizontal

English edition | by Cristina Berna and Eric Thomsen

3.1*3.1 out of 5 stars* (2)

Paperback

€35.73 €35.73

Get it **Tuesday, 2 May Wednesday, 24 May**

FREE Delivery

Hokusai 53 Stations of the Tōkaidō 1805-1806: Hardcover

English edition | by Cristina Berna and Eric Thomsen

1.0*1.0 out of 5 stars* (1)

Hardcover

€187.75 €187.75

Get it **Tuesday, 2 May** - **Wednesday, 24 May**

FREE Delivery

Kunisada 53 Stations of the Tōkaidō: Premium

English edition | by Cristina Berna and Eric Thomsen

3.0*3.0 out of 5 stars* (2)

Hardcover

€226.72 €226.72

Get it **Tuesday, 2 May** - **Wednesday, 24 May**

FREE Delivery

Hokusai 53 Stations of the Tōkaidō 1802: Premium

English edition | by Cristina Berna and Eric Thomsen

No reviews

Hardcover

€36.09 €36.09

Get it **Tuesday, 2 May** - **Wednesday, 24 May**

FREE Delivery

Joaquín Sorolla Portraits 3

English edition | by Cristina Berna and Eric Thomsen

1.0*1.0 out of 5 stars* (1)

Paperback

€34.02 €34.02

Get it **Thursday, 27 Apr** - **Monday, 22 May**

FREE Delivery

Yoshitaki Kunikazu Nansuitei Yoshiyuki 100 Views of Osaka: Hardcover

English edition | by Cristina Berna and Eric Thomsen

5.0*5.0 out of 5 stars* (1)

Hardcover

€277.31 €277.31

Get it **Tuesday, 2 May** - **Wednesday, 24 May**

FREE Delivery

Hiroshige Kunisada Kuniyoshi 53 Pairings of the Tōkaidō

English edition | by Cristina Berna and Eric Thomsen

3.0*3.0 out of 5 stars* (1)

Paperback

€137.75 €137.75

Get it **Thursday, 27 Apr** - **Monday, 22 May**

FREE Delivery

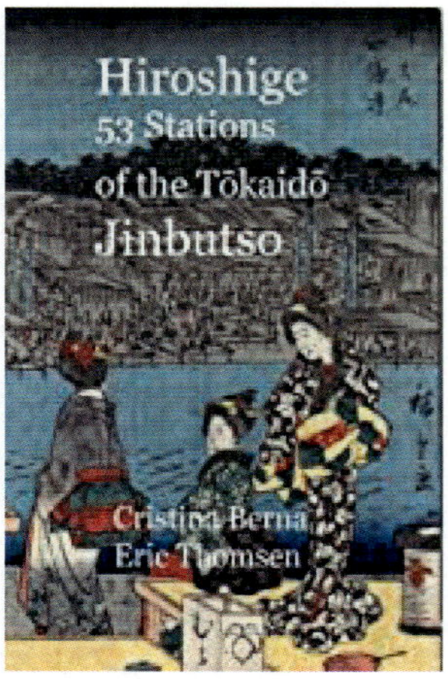

Hiroshige 53 Stations of the Tōkaidō Jinbutso

English edition | by Cristina Berna and Eric Thomsen

2.0*2.0 out of 5 stars* (5)

Paperback

€36.98 €36.98

Get it **Thursday, 27 Apr - Monday, 22 May**

FREE Delivery

Yamato Meisho Zue Vol 4 Rito Akisato Shunchosai Takehara 1791

English edition | by Cristina Berna and Eric Thomsen

No reviews

Paperback

€38.90 €38.90

Get it **Thursday, 27 Apr - Monday, 22 May**

FREE Delivery

Hiroshige 53 Stations of the Tōkaidō Aritaya

English edition | by Cristina Berna and Eric Thomsen

No reviews

Paperback

€37.14 €37.14

Get it **Thursday, 27 Apr** - **Monday, 22 May**

FREE Delivery

Tōkaidō Meisho Zue Vol 3 Rito Akisato Shunchosai Takehara 1797

English edition | by Cristina Berna and Eric Thomsen

No reviews

Paperback

€42.57 €42.57

Get it **Thursday, 27 Apr** - **Monday, 22 May**

FREE Delivery

Previous 1 2 Next

DO YOU NEED HELP?

RESULTS

Learn about these results.

Hiroshige 53 Stations of the Tōkaidō Kyōka: Premium

English edition | by Cristina Berna and Eric Thomsen

No reviews

Hardcover

€86.44 €86.44

Get it **Thursday, 27 Apr** - **Monday, 22 May**

FREE Delivery

Previous 1 **2** Next

Just a note about prices – which some reviewers have complained about –

Paragon is charging

New

€173.02 €173.02

for our German version of Joaquin Sorolla Familie, which we have listed at €99.95 via our agent.

This means when you read reviews of prices you can´t be sure what price the reviewer actually paid – was it list price, was it a hugely discounted price for a counterfeit copy or was it a speculation price?

You also note the long delivery time – these books are HANDMADE, to be sure….

Sorry, this was a long detour – we are going through the first 16 books we have uploaded to our agent, re-issuing titles that were "cancelled" by Ingram – here is no 3:

[Hiroshige 36 Vistas de Mo nte Fuji 1858]

Cristina Berna Precio 79.95€ ISBN 978-1-956773-83-5

This version was uploaded with our agent in Sevilla 9 November 2022, having been banned by Ingram – "cancelled" as they wrote, for abt two years. We were banned from making money on our own books, only Amazon making money on our name, by selling the "unavailable" books though Amazon itself and its "trusted sellers" like Bigly Books.

This book*, Hiroshige 36 Vistas de Monte Fuji 1858* is a series of Japanese prints with commentary, like the previous title, *Hiroshige 36 Views of Monte Fuji 1852*.

Hiroshige is one of the absolute masters of Japanese prints in the late Edo period. Hiroshige had an enormous influence on European painters like van Gogh. The authors have written a book also about van Gogh – Van Gogh Landscapes – The Japanese Connection – with ISBN number 978-1-960269-2-63 and available through the channels of our agent.

Hiroshige 36 Views of Monte Fuji 1988 also has a book page with Amazon.es according to our internal records in our agent:

Enlaces

Plataforma	Enlace
ama	https://www.amazon.es/s/ref=nb_sb_noss?__mk_es_ES=%C3%85M%C3%85%C5%BD%C3%95%C3%91&url=search-alias%3Daps&field-keywords=9781956773835

If you click the link you get again the message

Utilice menos palabras clave o pruebe con estas
No hay resultados para 9781956773835.

If you search amazon.com again with author+specific title you get the following message

one result for **"cristina berna hiroshige 36 vistas de monte fuji 1858"**

Sort by:

Featured

Sort by: Featured

RESULTS

Learn about these results.

Hiroshige 36 Vistas De Monte Fuji 1858: Hardcover

Spanish edition | by Cristina Berna and Eric Thomsen | 27 Mar 2020

No reviews

Hardcover

Currently unavailable.

Paperback

Currently unavailable.

The link (6 Apr 2023) is:

https://www.amazon.de/s?k=cristina+berna+hiroshige+36+vistas+de+monte+fuji+1858&crid=2UNXH5EME27N0&sprefix=cristina+berna+hiroshige+36+vistas+de+monte+fuji+1858%2Caps%2C123&ref=nb_sb_noss

Hiroshige 36 Vistas De Monte Fuji 1858: Hardcover Hardcover – Illustrated, 27 Mar. 2020

Spanish edition by Cristina Berna (Autor), Eric Thomsen (Autor)

No reviews

See all formats and editions

- **Hardcover**
  —
- Paperback
  —

Product details

- **Publisher** : Missys Clan; Illustrated edition (27 Mar. 2020)
- **Language** : Spanish
- **Hardcover** : 114 pages
- **ISBN-10** : 1648260454
- **ISBN-13** : 978-1648260452
- **Dimensions** : 15.19 x 1.12 x 22.91 cm

The ISBN number is one we purchased from ISBN Services Inc In New York.

It was used for this version uploaded to Ingram 27 Mar 2020 and "cancelled" abt July 2021.

As Amazon appears to write here, the book is "unavailable" in both hardcover and paperback.

But notice the small link

See all formats and editions

(enlarged here...)

If you click on that you get, first, a drop down no 1 on the hardcover version, no link provided:

2 formats and editions How are results ordered?

- **Hardcover, Illustrated (1)**
- Paperback, Illustrated (1)

Hiroshige 36 Vistas De Monte Fuji 1858: Hardcover

-

Rating	(0)
ISBN-13	978-1648260452
Publisher	Missys Clan
Edition	Illustrated

The ISBN number is the same as in the main page.

If you move to option (2) you get this drop down:

2 formats and editions How are results ordered?

- Hardcover, Illustrated (1)
- **Paperback, Illustrated (1)**

Hiroshige 36 Vistas De Monte Fuji 1858

-

Rating (0)

ISBN-13	**978-1648260292**
Publisher	Missys Clan
Edition	Illustrated
Publication Date	27 Mar. 2020

This is also our ISBN number, for the paperback, and also purchased from ISBN Services Inc in New York.

If you click on the title you are led to this page

https://www.amazon.de/-/en/Cristina-Berna/dp/1648260292/ref=monarch_sidesheet

Hiroshige 36 Vistas De Monte Fuji 1858 Paperback – Illustrated, 27 Mar. 2020

Spanish edition by Cristina Berna (Autor), Eric Thomsen (Autor)

No reviews

See all formats and editions

- Hardcover
  —
- **Paperback**
  —

.....

Product details

- **Publisher** : Missys Clan; Illustrated edition (27 Mar. 2020)
- **Language** : Spanish
- **Paperback** : 114 pages
- **ISBN-10** : 1648260292
- **ISBN-13** : 978-1648260292
- **Dimensions** : 15.19 x 0.61 x 22.91 cm

We therefore ask ourselves – have these two books been *banned* from Amazon, and for what reason??

We have done nothing wrong.

Amazon is showing – via our agent - the books have a link in Amazon.es but the link is not opening anything for the potential buyer, meaning Amazon is in effect blocking the books.

Amazon and Ingram have near monopoly in the EU except for Spain and near monopoly in the US and elsewhere. This has a huge social impact on the authors.

Take then the fourth book we were able to upload with Our agent CC in Sevilla

Gatos en el arte

Cristina Berna Precio 99.95€ ISBN 978-1-956773-84-2

This book was also uploaded 9 Nov 2022

This book also has a book page in Amazon.es according to our agent:

Enlaces

Plataforma	Enlace
ama	https://www.amazon.es/s/ref=nb_sb_noss?__mk_es_ES=%C3%85M%C3%85%C5%BD%C3%95%C3%91&url=search-alias%3Daps&field-keywords=9781956773842

This is the first book out of four that has proper information in Amazon.es

Resultados

Más información sobre estos resultados.

Gatos en el arte: Línea de tiempo

de Cristina Berna y Eric Thomsen

Sin reseñas

Tapa blanda

99,95 € 99,95€

Entrega por 5,71 € el **ju., 6 de abr.**

This book is also the first which has proper search results in amazon.com

https://www.amazon.com/s?k=cristina+berna+gatos&i=stripbooks-intl-ship&crid=1ERUFVV3IFVAR&sprefix=cristina+berna+gatos%2Cstripbooks-intl-ship%2C330&ref=nb_sb_noss

RESULTS

...

2 resultados para "cristina berna+gatos en el arte"

Ordenar por:

Lanzamientos recientes

Ordenar por: Destacados

Resultados

Más información sobre estos resultados.

Gatos en el arte: Línea de tiempo
de Cristina Berna y Eric Thomsen

Sin reseñas

Tapa blanda

99,95 € 99,95€

Entrega por 5,71 € el **mi., 12 de abr.**

Hiroshige 36 Vistas de Monte Fuji 1852: Premium

de Cristina Berna y Eric Thomsen

Sin reseñas

Tapa dura

No disponible.

Otro formato: Tapa blanda

Link to these two results amazon.es (6 Apr 2023):

https://www.amazon.es/s?k=cristina+berna%2Bgatos+en+el+arte&__mk_es_ES=%C3%85M%C3%85%C5%BD%C3%95%C3%91&crid=28KVJFPBY4A08&sprefix=cristina+berna+gatos+en+el+arte%2Caps%2C128&ref=nb_sb_noss

Let us first look at result no 2 – for *Hiroshige 36 Vistas de Monte Fuji 1852*.

Above we saw that Amazon.com offered this "unavailable" version with the Ingram ISBN for €62.14 and Amazon´s "trusted seller" Bigly Books offered the same version for €134.68.

But both offers are "unavailable". Ingram assured us that no book would be printed except when a copy was ordered from an independent bookstore and paid by the customer. They were POD – Print on Demand. These appear to be **new** books. Where do Amazon and Bigly get them?

Until Ingram "cancelled" all our 291 titles abt two years ago, we received monthly sales statements with ISBN numbers and accrued author´s fees.

After Ingram suddenly "cancelled" all our titles, we didn´t receive sales reports for further sales and certainly no sales reports or accrued author´s fees statements from either Amazon or Bigly Books or any other "trusted seller".

What did Ingram do with our pdf files for cover and interior, for each of the 291 titles?

Ingram has never explained anything to us about what they did with the copyrighted books and the pdf files they used, to print them after, each time a customer ordered a copy.

We have not signed any agreements to transfer these files to third parties.

They have not become Ingram´s property because we didn´t pick them up within 90 days – as with a certain laptop.

The whole book business is developing more and more towards printing small runs of books down to one at a time.

We have no information that Amazon has gone the other way and purchased huge runs of our books at full price and stored them in enormous warehouses for many years, from where they are now sold at discount prices surely causing alarming losses for Amazon?

We don´t think this is what is taking place.

We believe that Amazon and its "trusted sellers" obtain the Ingram books from someone – perhaps Ingram or perhaps from someone with access to the pdfs.

Go back now to the Hiroshige 1852 from the search results in Spanish amazon.es

Hiroshige 36 Vistas de Monte Fuji 1852 Tapa blanda – 12 febrero 2020

de Cristina Berna (Autor)

Sin reseñas

Ver todos los formatos y ediciones

- Tapa dura
  115,74 €
  Otros nuevo a partir de 115,74 €
- **Tapa blanda**
  —

https://www.amazon.es/Hiroshige-Vistas-Monte-Fuji-

1852/dp/1647862981/ref=sr_1_2?__mk_es_ES=%C3%85M%C3%85%C5%BD%C3%95%C3%91&crid=28KVJFPBY4A08&keywords=cristina+berna%2Bgatos+en+el+arte&qid=1680790199&sprefix=cristina+berna+gatos+en+el+arte%2Caps%2C128&sr=8-2

On this search amazon provides a result from amazon.es instead of amazon.de and now the hardback version – the "unavailable" Ingram hardback version is offered at €115.74

If you click the "other versions" link, you get a drop-down stating the seller is Amazon itself.

We have no information from Amazon how many copies they have sold since abt July 2021, when Ingram "cancelled" this title and we have no statement of accrued author´s fees from either Amazon or Ingram for these sales.

Hiroshige 36 Vistas de Monte Fuji 1852
Tapa dura

Nuevo
115,74 € 115,74€

Entrega por 5,69 € el **sábado, 15 de abril**. Ver detalles

Submit Añadir a la cesta

Envía por

Amazon

Vendedor

Amazon

Ver menos

Actualmente no hay ofertas de otros vendedores que coincidan con tu ubicación o con las especificaciones del producto. Intenta actualizar los filtros o la ubicación.

Filtrar (1)

Nuevo

You will note that Amazon states the book is "new" – "Nuevo". OK, we have highlighted this with yellow, but that does not change Amazon´s claim that this is a new book. It is not a book they bought more than two years ago….

This is a new book Amazon is offering for sale, and it bears the ISBN number 978-1-647862-98-5 which is associated with this title in the Ingram version and which was "cancelled" abt two years ago.

This is an ISBN number we purchased and paid for from ISBN Services Inc in New York.

This is our property. This is our book. This is our work product. This is our labor. We had a contract with Ingram, who baited us to self-publish with them, claiming they would distribute World Wide through at that time some 39,000 book stores.

And then suddenly for no good reason Ingram "cancelled" all our 291 titles and now Amazon sells them "new".

We can show you emails from Ingram that they approved each and every single title before it was published to the bookstores.

How can Ingram then "cancel" these approved books and let Amazon use the files without paying author´s fees?

Let us look now at the other search result, for "*Gatos en el Arte*", the fourth book we uploaded to our agent.

If you click on this title, you get the following link:

https://www.amazon.es/"Gatos-arte-tiempo-Cristina-Berna/dp/1956773843/ref=sr_1_1?__mk_es_ES=%C3%85M%C3%85%C5%BD%C3%95%C3%91&crid=28KVJFPBY4A08&keywords=cristina+berna%2Bgatos+en+el+arte&qid=1680792381&sprefix=cristina+berna+gatos+en+el+arte%2Caps%2C128&sr=8-1

This link shows you the following information:

Gatos en el arte: Línea de tiempo Tapa blanda – 9 noviembre 2022

de Cristina Berna (Autor), Eric Thomsen (Autor)

Sin reseñas

Ver todos los formatos y ediciones

- **Tapa blanda**
  99,95 €
  Otros nuevo a partir de 99,95 €

Durante

Detalles del producto

- **Editorial** : VESTERNAES (9 noviembre 2022)
- **Idioma** : Español
- **Tapa blanda** : 220 páginas
- **ISBN-10** : 1956773843
- **ISBN-13** : 978-1956773842
- **Peso del producto** : 349 g
- **Dimensiones** : 14 x 1.27 x 21.6 cm

This is all correct information.

This shows you that Amazon of course is capable of doing things right. Amazon can show you the right information when it wants to. This is not a technical problem, it is not a mess created by unions or daft subcontractors or whatever excuse you can get. The Amazon people are very capable and methodical. They have to be to run that huge website and operation.

But there does not exist a "cancelled" Spanish version with an Ingram ISBN number.

Take good note of that.

The number above, ISBN 978-1-956773-84-2 is an ISBN number is one we have purchased and paid for from Bowker, the official ISBN agency in the United States.

We do not know, of course, whether Amazon is reporting and paying for all copies printed with this number and sold through our agent to Amazon.

In effect we do not know if we get all the author´s fees which are calculated in our agent´s website.

Let us go now to the fifth book we have uploaded to Our agent CC.

Cristina Berna Precio 79.95€ ISBN 978-1-956773-88-0

The fifth book was uploaded 15 Nov 2022

It has a book page link
in amazon.es according to Our agent CC

Plataforma	Enlace
	https://www.amazon.es/s/ref=nb_sb_noss?__mk_es_ES=%C3%85M%C3%85%C5%BD%C3%95%C3%91&url=search-alias%3Daps&field-keywords=9781956773880

If you click on this link you get the following information:

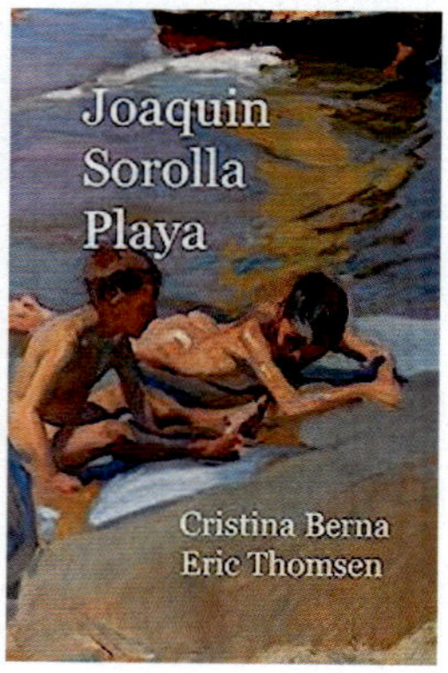

Joaquin Sorolla Playa

de Cristina Berna y Eric Thomsen

2.0 *2,0 de 5 estrellas* (1)

Tapa blanda

79,95 € 79,95€

Entrega por 5,66 € el **ju., 6 de abr.**

Entrega más rápida el **mi., 5 de abr.**

Más opciones de compra
74,35 € (2 ofertas usadas y nuevas)

For the first time we see the link to "other purchase options" – "Más opciones de compra" directly in the link for the re-issued title we have uploaded through our agent after Ingram abt two years ago "cancelled" all our 291 titles for no good reason after having approved them all in writing.

If you click this link you get a drop-down showing the following:

Joaquin Sorolla Playa
Tapa blanda

1 valoración

Nuevo
79,95 €   79,95€

Entrega por 5,66 € el **jueves, 6 de abril**. Haz el pedido en 14 horas 5 mins. Ver detalles

entrega más rápida el **miércoles, 5 de abril**. Ver detalles

Submit Añadir a la cesta

Envía por

Amazon

Vendedor

Amazon

Ver menos

1 opción más

De 2ª mano - Muy bueno

74,35 € 74,35€

Entrega por 5,66 € el **jueves, 6 de abril**. Haz el pedido en 20 mins. Ver detalles

Submit Añadir a la cesta

Estado

Falta el envoltorio de plástico, pueden faltar los códigos de activación para el contenido adicional en... Más

Envía por

Amazon

Vendedor

Amazon Warehouse

Fin de los resultados

How can it be there are already "used" copies in good quality on offer?

We know that Amazon offers buyers a 30 day return, and apparently this is what could be the explanation? Or?

We have no information how many copies of the title has been sold. Compared to Ingram who gave us monthly sales data within eight days of a month ending. Amazon is not providing us any sales data and not any data on accrued author´s fees.

There is one review of this book – but from the United States:

Reseñas más importantes de otros países

Traducir todas las opiniones al español

htherschel

2,0 de 5 estrellas **Terrible book about a great painter**

Revisado en los Estados Unidos el 31 de mayo de 2021

Compra verificada

Terrible prints of his work!! Not worth the cost

The review claims the print is poor.

This is not the first time customers on Amazon complain about the print.

We never had a complaint from Ingram.

We do not know, of course, whether Ingram printed this book. The review is dated 31 May 2021 – this is shortly before Ingram "cancelled" all our 291 titles.

We hear that Amazon itself prints the copies it sells of the new versions we have uploaded.

This means the authors have no control over print quality.

The authors have not heard any complaints from our agent over print quality from the other channels the book is distributed to.

It could be that the book was a counterfeit or that the print quality was really very bad? The dirt is on the authors.

If you click on the "other formats available" there is a drop-down with the following information:

1 formatos y ediciones¿Cómo se ordenan los resultados?

- **Tapa blanda (1)**

Joaquin Sorolla Playa

79,95 €   €79,95

Nuevo desde 79,95 €

De 2ª mano desde 74,35 €

Calificación	(0)
ISBN-13	978-1956773880
Fecha de publicación	15 noviembre 2022

If you instead do a search on Amazon Books, author+title specific, you get this result:

First, here is the link (6 Apr 2023)

https://www.amazon.com/Joaqu%C3%ADn-Sorolla-Beach-Cristina-Berna/dp/2919787683/ref=sr_1_2?crid=3Q4TYY6D32EVK&keywords=cristina+berna+joaquin+sorolla+playa&qid=1680509055&s=books&sprefix=cristina+berna+joaquin+sorolla+playa%2Cstripbooks-intl-ship%2C238&sr=1-2

The search does not provide the Spanish edition uploaded via our agent, but instead cuts to the English language "cancelled" Ingram version.

Look inside

Joaquín Sorolla Beach Taschenbuch – 17. August 2019

von Cristina Berna (Author), Eric Thomsen (Author)

1,0 von 5 Sternen 2 Sternebewertungen

Alle Formate und Editionen anzeigen

- Taschenbuch

—

Produktinformation

- **Herausgeber :** Missys Clan (17. August 2019)
- **Sprache :** Englisch
- **Taschenbuch :** 156 Seiten
- **ISBN-10 :** 2919787683
- **ISBN-13 :** 978-2919787685
- **Artikelgewicht :** 218 g
- **Abmessungen :** 15.19 x 0.84 x 22.91 cm
- **Amazon Bestseller-Rang:** Nr. 6,104,481 in Bücher (Siehe Top 100 in Bücher)
  - Nr. 27,718 in Kunstkritik
  - Nr. 104,408 in Europäische Geschichte (Bücher)
  - Nr. 181,022 in Reisen & Tourismus (Bücher)
- **Kundenrezensionen:**
  *1,0 von 5 Sternen*_ 2 Sternebewertungen

We hope it does not bother you that some of the information is in German.

In this search we get two other, different reviews:

Spitzenbewertung aus USA

Alle Rezensionen ins Deutsche übersetzen

C&C

1,0 von 5 Sternen **Not really a book.**

Kundenrezension aus den USA us am 5. Januar 2020

Verifizierter Kauf

Looks like it might have been a dissertation that was "published" through Amazon. Very disappointing for the price as other texts are much better made and presented.

2 Personen fanden diese Informationen hilfreich

Diese Bewertung als hilfreich markieren BUTTON

Nützlich

Melden

Rezensionen auf Deutsch übersetzen

Alle Rezensionen anzeigen

Spitzenrezensionen aus anderen Ländern

Alle Rezensionen ins Deutsche übersetzen

David

1,0 von 5 Sternen **Not up to standard**

Kundenrezension aus Großbritannien GB am 19. September 2019

Verifizierter Kauf

I have had to return my copy. It is a flimsy publication using low-grade paper, and consequently the quality of the pictures is simply not good enough. At a quick glance, the commentary seems aimed at children or students. The price is just ludicrous. There are far better books on Sorolla on the market.

Melden

Rezensionen auf Deutsch übersetzen

It is not possible for the authors to give feedback on the Amazon site. It is only the customer, who can say anything. The author can not defend him- or herself.

Here is a chance to comment, though:

First, C&C: there are many "dissertations" which are being published on "Amazon".

This book was published on Ingram and apparently sold on Amazon. We bought many text books earlier, when Amazon was younger. This means the reviewer acknowledges the quality of the work as textbook or is criticising the education system...

But, no. This is not a “dissertation”. It was admittedly the first book we did on Joaquin Sorolla and his wonderful paintings.

Second, the remark on texts “better made and presented” may be due to the profile the authors have published. Of course, everyone can get better and that is a great effect of reviews. They point to how you may get better. But t just here are many very vile “reviews” on Amazon which are not really reviews but a chance to vent and vomit.

As for price, we write for a living. We don´t have a university to fund the printing nor do we have a university job to pay for our daily bread. That is why we are writing this book about many copies of our books apparently being sold without any author´s fees being sent our way. They take our bread and eat it.

Second, David: Yes, Ingram offered three quality levels – paperback, hardback and premium. Each version had different prices. We strove on Ingram to make all three versions for all titles so it would be up to the customer to decide, what quality he wanted to pay for.

David says the text is "aimed for children or students".

This indicates David is in a higher learning institution or perhaps a museum in Britain. Our books are aimed at the general public, "the trade".

We do have better reviews for some of the other titles that Ingram "cancelled". Some titles received five stars out of five.

Again, poor paper and print quality is a function of price and we do not appear to control this parameter completely. David appears to have purchased the poorest quality, the paperback.

Above you saw how Amazon was able to sell our title "*Luxembourg – un morceau de gâteau*" French version, for €4.55 which is far below what we are charged for the printing – but Amazon does not pay us anything. How is the print here?

It is our opinion that a writer of such narrow titles as we produce should not work for free.

Not everyone shares this opinion.

If you click on the link for "see all purchase options" -

Alle Formate und Editionen anzeigen

You get a drop down with this information (there is no link to the drop-down):

(6 Apr 2023):

- **Taschenbuch (2)**

Joaquín Sorolla Beach

52,45$ $52,45

Neu ab 5245 $

Bewertung	(0)
ISBN-13	9781960269003
Veröffentlichungsdatum	Dezember 28, 2022

Joaquín Sorolla Beach

-

Bewertung	(2)
ISBN-13	9782919787685
Verlag	Missys Clan
Veröffentlichungsdatum	August 17, 2019

The ISBN number was issued by the national ISBN agency in Luxembourg. The number for the "cancelled" Ingram paperback ISBN 978-2919787685 was also issued by Luxembourg. The number for the paperback in the drop down is the Bowker number for the re-issued version.

The sixth book we uploaded to our agent was:

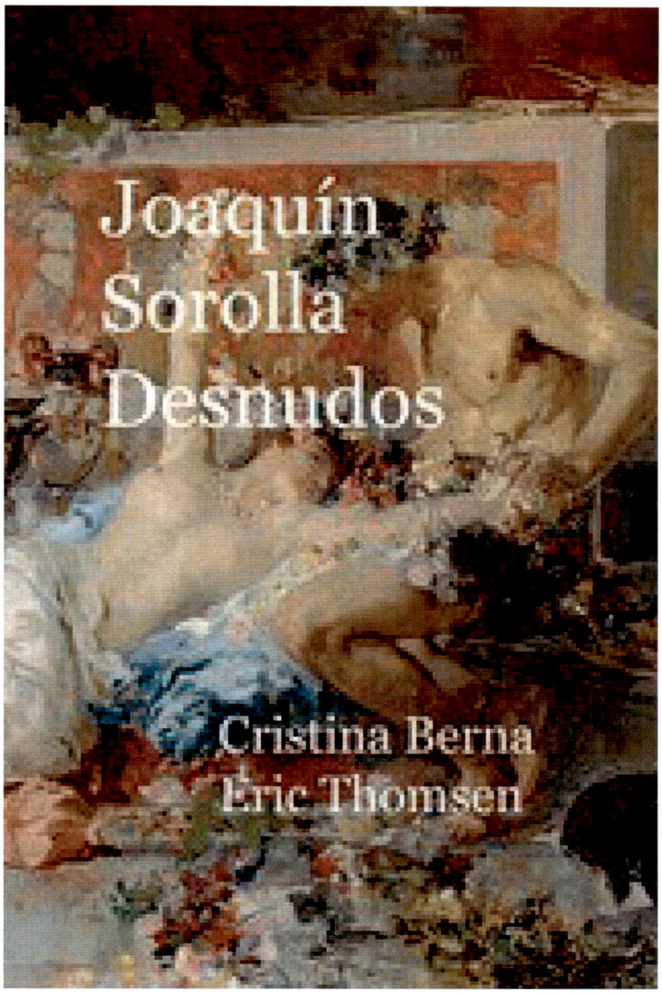

Joaquín Sorolla Desnudos

Cristina Berna Precio 79.95€ ISBN 978-1-956773-90-3

This book was uploaded 27 Nov 2023

The book has a link to a book page with amazon.es, according to our agent:

Enlaces

Plataforma	Enlace
	https://www.amazon.es/s/ref=nb_sb_noss?__mk_es_ES=%C3%85M%C3%85%C5%BD%C3%95%C3%91&url=search-alias%3Daps&field-keywords=9781956773903

If you click the link you get this information:

Joaquín Sorolla Desnudos

de Cristina Cristina Berna y Eric Thomsen

Sin reseñas

Tapa blanda

79,95 € 79,95€

Entrega por 5,68 € el **ju., 6 de abr.**

which is correct.

If you search amazon.com

author+title specific you get this result:

RESULTS

Joaquín Sorolla Desnudos (Spanish Edition)

Spanish Edition | by Cristina Cristina Berna and Eric Thomsen | Nov 27, 2022

No reviews

Paperback

$84.90 $84.90

Delivery **Fri, Apr 21**

Or fastest delivery **Thu, Apr 13**

Ships to Austria

Joaquín Sorolla Nudes

by Cristina Berna and Eric Thomsen | Aug 18, 2019

1.4*1.4 out of 5 stars* [(3)]

Paperback

Currently unavailable.

Use fewer keywords or try these instead

The link was (4 Apr 2023)

https://www.amazon.com/s?k=cristina+berna+Joaqu%C3%ADn+Sorolla+Desnudos&i=stripbooks-intl-ship&crid=13NQYHMNKR17U&sprefix=cristina+berna+joaqu%C3%ADn+sorolla+desnudos%2Cstripbooks-intl-ship%2C371&ref=nb_sb_noss

Again, the Spanish version information is correct,

but Amazon is listing the English version as unavailable which is incorrect and this may surely depress sales.

On 6 Apr 2023 the link was

https://www.amazon.es/s?k=cristina+berna+joaquin+sorolla+desnudos&__mk_es_ES=%C3%85M%C3%85%C5%BD%C3%95%C3%91&crid=2KHKZKB07QQKD&sprefix=cristina+berna+joaquin+sorolla+desnudos%2Caps%2C127&ref=nb_sb_noss

and now the English language version uploaded through our agent is shown, with correct price:

Joaquín Sorolla Desnudos

de Cristina Cristina Berna y Eric Thomsen

Sin reseñas

Tapa blanda

79,95 €   79,95€

Entrega por 5,68 € el **ju., 13 de abr.**

Entrega más rápida el **mi., 12 de abr.**

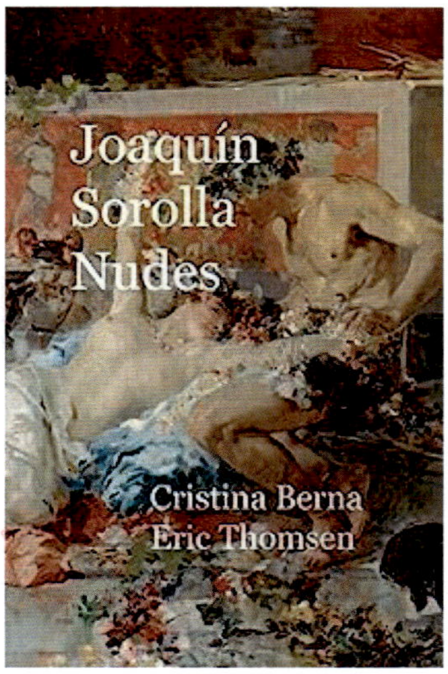

Joaquín Sorolla Nudes

Edición en Inglés

de Cristina Berna

1,4*1,4 de 5 estrellas* (3)

Tapa blanda

79,95 €   79,95€

Entrega por 5,68 € el **mi., 12 de abr.**

The Spanish version has never been available on Ingram, and was thus not "cancelled". It appears for the first time.

There are no revies on the Spanish version.

There is a review from Spain apparently from a customer to the English language version ISBN 978-1-956773-93-4. The review is in Portuguese.

Principal reseña de España

Filipe Chelles Ieker

1,0 de 5 estrellas **Qualidade da impressão**

Revisado en España el 17 de diciembre de 2022

Compra verificada

A qualidade da impressão é muito ruim. As imagens foram retiradas de sites na Internet. Não são fotografias originais de obras do artista. Decepcionado.

Translation:

Print quality is very poor. The images were taken from websites on the Internet. They are not original photographs of the artist's works. Disappointed.

Again, here is a complaint about print quality and we asked our agent about it, because the Ingram versions except perhaps sometimes for the cheapest paperback didn´t give rise to complaints over print quality. We got the explanation that the printing was done by Amazon.

As for the images taken from the internet, this is completely true and cited in the photo credits.

Granted there are a few images which were of poorer quality, but generally you are able to find good quality images that print very well, if you have good printers. This customer Is apparently not aware of this. Note, however that the customer does not complain about the text, that it is for children or students.

Reviews are very, very important for many customers in the decision to buy or not to buy -

There is a second review from a customer in the United States:

Ohad Schutz

2,0 de 5 estrellas **Low quality images**

Revisado en los Estados Unidos el 17 de junio de 2021

Compra verificada

Low quality of images

A una persona le ha parecido esto útil

Denunciar

Traducir reseña a Español

Again, this reviewer complains about the poor quality of the images.

The authors strive to use the best available images. It is always distressing to have dissatisfied customers. However, the authors do not control print quality when the books are sold via Amazon. Amazon does not allow the authors to reply on the Amazon website and it is very difficult to contact Amazon if you are not buying something.

The seventh book we have already briefly touched upon:

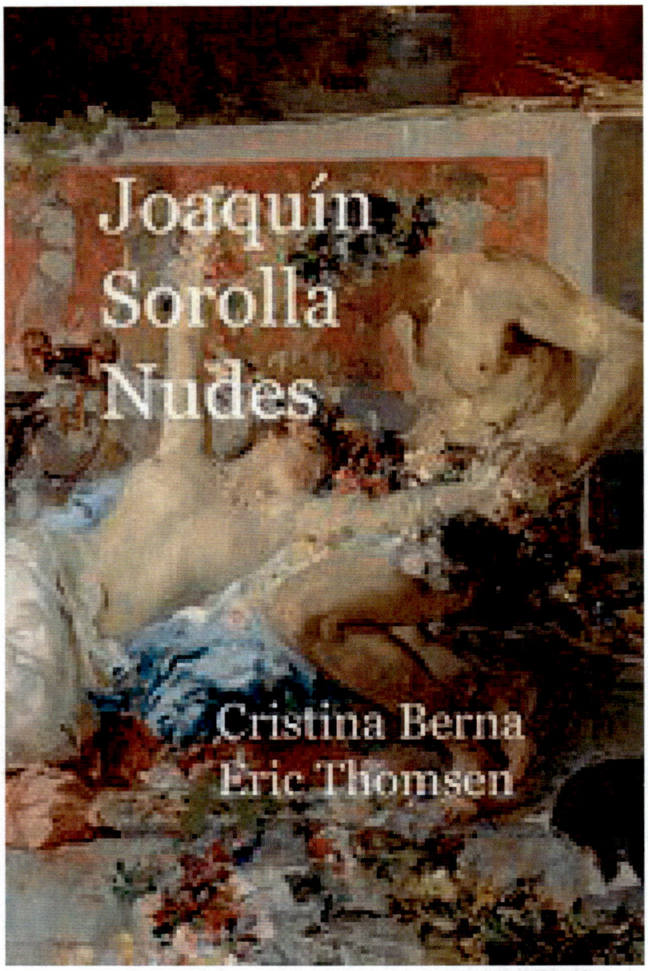

Joaquín Sorolla Nudes

Cristina Berna Precio 79.95€ ISBN 978-1-956773-93-4

This English version was uploaded 15 Dec 2022 to our agent and that (6 Apr 2023) is well over three months ago, so there is no serious excuse that Amazon has not had time to update its databases.

According to our agent this English version has a book page with amazon.es

Enlaces

Plataforma	Enlace
ama	https://www.amazon.es/s/ref=nb_sb_noss?__mk_es_ES=%C3%85M%C3%85%C5%BD%C3%95%C3%91&url=search-alias%3Daps&field-keywords=9781956773934

and if you click the link you get this result

Joaquín Sorolla Nudes

Edición en Inglés

de Cristina Berna

1.4*1,4 de 5 estrellas* (3)

Tapa blanda

79,95 €79,95€

Entrega por 5,68 € el **ju., 6 de abr.**

Entrega más rápida el **mi., 5 de abr.**

This is the correct information.

In the author+title specific search on amazon.com, you get this result:

The link is:

https://www.amazon.com/s?k=cristina+berna+joaquin+Sorolla+nudes&i=stripbooks-intl-ship&__mk_de_DE=%C3%85M%C3%85%C5%BD%C3%95%C3%91&crid=27R8PPE9D51EF&sprefix=cristina+berna+joaquin+sorolla+n

udes%2Cstripbooks-intl-ship%2C339&ref=nb_sb_noss

The result gives links to other author´s books:

5 Ergebnisse für **"cristina berna joaquin Sorolla nudes"**
Sortieren nach:

Bestseller Sortieren nach:Amazon präsentiert

ERGEBNISSE

Joaquín Sorolla Nudes

von Cristina Berna | 15. Dezember 2022

1.4*1,4 von 5 Sternen* (3)

Taschenbuch

84,92$ 84,92$

Lieferung **Mi., 26. Apr.**

Oder schnellste Lieferung **Di., 18. Apr.**

Für Versand nach Österreich qualifiziert

Sorolla: The Masterworks

von Blanca Pons-Sorolla | 2. Oktober 2012

4.8*4,8 von 5 Sternen* (461)

[Gebundenes Buch]

48,49$ 48,49$

Lieferung **Mo., 24. Apr.**

Oder schne llste Lieferung **Mo., 17. Apr.**

Für Versand nach Österreich qualifiziert

Andere Angebote
32,98$ [(26 gebrauchte und neue Artikel)]

Joaquín Sorolla- The Paintings (Zedign Art Series)
von Joaquín Sorolla | 21. Juni 2017

3.4*3,4 von 5 Sternen* (7)

Kindle

7,44$ 7,44$

Sofort lieferbar

Taschenbuch

22,98$ 22,98$

Lieferung **Mo., 24. Apr.**

Oder schnellste Lieferung **Di., 18. Apr.**

Für Versand nach Österreich qualifiziert

Sorolla and the Paris Years

von Blanca Pons-Sorolla, Véronique Gerard-Powell, et al. | 3. Mai 2016

4.8*4,8 von 5 Sternen* (108)

[Gebundenes Buch](#)

42,67$ 42,67$

UVP: 50,00 $50,00$

Lieferung **Di., 25. Apr.**

Oder schnellste Lieferung **Di., 18. Apr.**

Für Versand nach Österreich qualifiziert

Nur noch 2 vorrätig – bestellen Sie bald.

Andere Angebote
21,44 $(43 gebrauchte und neue Artikel)

Spanish Painting 1665-1920 (Art Periods & Movements)
von Emma Hansen und Ruth Dangelmeier | 1. Januar 2020

4.8*4,8 von 5 Sternen* (16)

Gebundenes Buch

49,95$ 49,95$

Lieferung **Mo., 24. Apr.**

Oder schnellste Lieferung **Mo., 17. Apr.**

Für Versand nach Österreich qualifiziert

Andere Angebote
32,65 $ (15 gebrauchte und neue Artikel)

Flexible Bindung

16,95$ 16,95$

Lieferung **Mo., 24. Apr.**

Oder schnellste Lieferung **Mo., 17. Apr.**

Für Versand nach Österreich qualifiziert

Andere Angebote
14,77$ (32 gebrauchte und neue Artikel)

If the potential customer is searching for "themes" it is excellent to get other author´s works suggested.

But if you search a specific author or a specific author plus theme, why is Amazon suggesting other author´s works instead of other works by the searched author?

It appears like Amazon shunts queries away from the specific author and over to other authors. The authors are only allowed three search words, so how do these authors land here?

The eight book uploaded to our agent was:

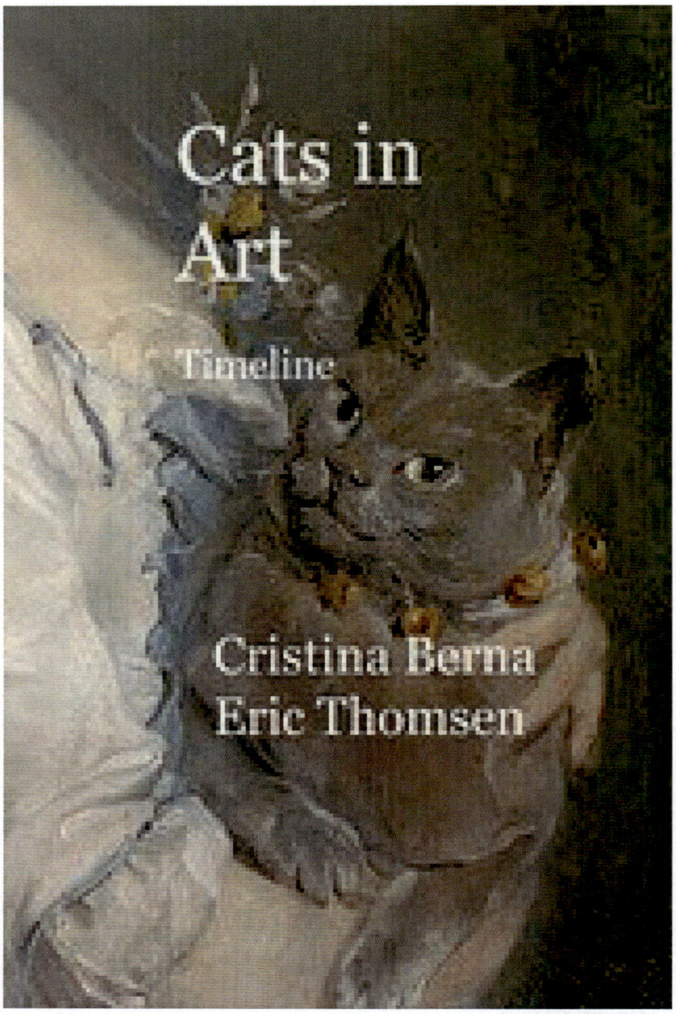

Cats in Art Timeline

Cristina Berna Precio 79.95€ ISBN 978-1-956773-94-1

This book was uploaded 15 Dec 2022 and

it has a book page link
in amazon.es according to our agent

Enlaces

Plataforma	Enlace
ama	https://www.amazon.es/s/ref=nb_sb_noss?__mk_es_ES=%C3%85M%C3%85%C5%BD%C3%95%C3%91&url=search-alias%3Daps&field-keywords=9781956773941

If you click this link, you get the following information:

Cats in Art Timeline
Edición en Inglés
de Cristina Berna

5.0*5,0 de 5 estrellas* (1)

Tapa blanda

79,95 € 79,95€

Entrega por 5,70 € el **ju., 6 de abr.**

Entrega más rápida el **mi., 5 de abr.**

which is correct information.

There is a link to other versions of this title:

Ver todos los formatos y ediciones

If you click this link, you get a drop-down, with no link.

- **Tapa blanda**
  (2)

Cats in Art Timeline

79,95€ €79,95

Nuevo desde 79,95 €

Calificación	(0)
ISBN-13	978-1956773941
Fecha de publicación	15 diciembre 2022

Cats in Art: Timeline

-

De coleccionista desde 107,48 €

Calificación	(1)
ISBN-13	978-2919787722

This is advertised as a "collector´s book". The price is well above the price for a new paperback via our agent. The ISBN number is from the national ISBN agency in Luxembourg.

But when a trader starts treating one of our books as a “collector´s item”, this put the bad reviews above in perspective.

If our books are worthy of being “collector´s items” this is a sort of praise that speaks of some consideration.

What we don´t know if this book is genuine or counterfeit. It does not say “new”.

Like in the art world – both with the Japanese prints we have written about and the Joaquin Sorolla paintings there are many forgeries.

We cite in one of our Sorolla books Blanca Pons-Sorolla, the eminent authority on her illustrious ancestor that she has recorded more than 2,000 fake “Sorolla” paintings.

By the way, please don´t complain about the “pixilated” pictures in this book....

You can now click on this link:

De coleccionista desde 107,48 €

You get a drop-down with this information:

De coleccionista - Bueno

107,48€ 107,48€

Entrega por 6,54 € entre el **8 - 16 de mayo**. Ver detalles

Submit Añadir a la cesta

Envía por

SonicBW

Vendedor

SonicBW

Nuevo vendedor

This is one of Amazon´s "trusted sellers" and he is "new". This is like an e-bay addition to Amazon´s own business.

If you click on this link inside the drop-down:

SonicBW

You get a link with the following information:

Información detallada sobre el vendedor
Vendedor comercial

Nombre de empresa: Guolian Wang

Tipo de empresa: Empresa privada

Número de registro mercantil: 621855347

Dirección empresarial:

18 Renata

NEWPORT COAST

CA

92657-1231

US

Link:

https://www.amazon.es/sp?ie=UTF8&seller=A1EKVJ5I701Z4E&isAmazonFulfilled=0&asin=2919787721&ref_=olp_merch_name_1

This “trusted seller” also has a storefront in Amazon.com

The link shows he is offering 100,000 books for sale, displayed 16 on each page. Of course he does not have 100,000 books in storage? They are printed as he needs them or perhaps drawn from a central storage with a few copies? What you don´t know is who prints the books and where do they get the pdf files for the cover and the interior?

Do they get them from Ingram?

Are any of these 100,000 books “cancelled” or “out of print”?

1-16 de más de 100.000 resultados

Ordenar por: Destacados Ordenar por:Destacados

Resultados

Más información sobre estos resultados.

Más vendido

El Hombre en busca de Sentido

de Viktor Emil Frankl, José Benigno Freire, et ál.

4,5*4,5 de 5 estrellas* (15.420) **Tapa blanda**

If you now search – on SonicBW´s storefront, the author Cristina Berna, you get the following result:

Resultados

Más información sobre estos resultados.

Christmas Nativity Salzburg: Hardcover

Edición en Inglés | de Cristina Berna y Eric Thomsen

Sin reseñas

Tapa dura

Christmas Market Salzburg: Hardcover

Edición en Inglés | de Cristina Berna y Eric Thomsen

2,5*2,5 de 5 estrellas* (2)

Tapa dura

Joaquín Sorolla Portraits 3: Hardcover

Edición en Inglés | de Cristina Berna y Eric Thomsen

1,0*1,0 de 5 estrellas* (1)

Tapa dura

Hiroshige 53 Stations of the Tōkaidō Kyōka: Premium

Edición en Inglés | de Cristina Berna y Eric Thomsen

Sin reseñas

Tapa dura

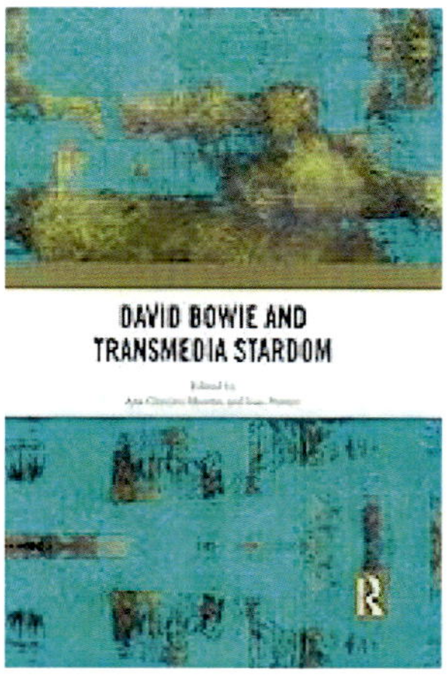

David Bowie and Transmedia Stardom

Edición en Inglés | de Ana Cristina Mendes y Lisa Perrott

Sin reseñas

Tapa blanda

We can´t comment on David Bowie´s book, but Christmas Market Salzburg, Christmas Market Salzburg, Joaquin Sorolla Portraits 3 and Hiroshige 53 Stations of the Tokaido Kyoka are all "cancelled" by Ingram and should not be available for sale.

If you click on the link for "Christmas Market Salzburg," åublished 15 Mar 2019 you get this drop-down:

Christmas Nativity Salzburg: Hardcover
Tapa dura

---

1 opción
ordenado por precio + envío: de menor a mayor

Filtrar (1)

De coleccionista

Borrar todo

De coleccionista - Bueno
50,97 €50,97€

Entrega por 6,63 € entre el **8 - 16 de mayo**. Ver detalles

Submit Añadir a la cesta

Envía por

SonicBW

Vendedor

SonicBW

Nuevo vendedor

Fin de los resultados

The seller is SonicBW. The ISBN is 978-2919787982, which is one of our ISBN numbers from Luxembourg.

There is a dash for “paperback” – tapa blanda – this is ISBN 978-2919787593, another of our numbers from the National ISBN number provider in Luxembourg.

Click the “ver mas” – show more, and a drop-down tells you the seller is – Amazon:

Christmas Nativity Salzburg
Tapa blanda

Nuevo
48,85€ 48,85€

Entrega por 5,66 € el **jueves, 13 de abril**. Ver detalles

Submit Añadir a la cesta

Envía por

Amazon

Vendedor

Amazon

Ver menos

And Amazon is offering this “unavailable” book “cancelled” by Ingram abt two years ago – for no good reason – for €48.85.

How is this possible?

How can Amazon sell a “new” book which was not printed for more than two years – according to Ingram – if they don´t have access to the pdf files that were uploaded to Ingram?

How did Amazon get access to these files which Ingram was supposed to guard?

If you click on the link for "Christmas Market Salzburg", published 11 Mar 2019, you get a drop-down with this result:

Christmas Market Salzburg: Hardcover

Tapa dura

2 valoraciones

De 2ª mano - Bueno

76,61€ 76,61€

Entrega por 6,99 € entre el **3 - 24 de mayo**. Ver detalles

Submit Añadir a la cesta

Ver más

---

1 opción más
ordenado por precio + envío: de menor a mayor

Filtrar (4)

De 2ª mano - Como nuevo

De 2ª mano - Muy bueno

+2

Borrar todo

De 2ª mano - Bueno

79,61€ 79,61€

Entrega por 15,69 € entre el **19 de mayo - 9 de junio**. Ver detalles

Submit Añadir a la cesta

Envía por

BEANNY

Vendedor

BEANNY

(332 calificaciones)
72 % positivas en los últimos 12 meses

Fin de los resultados

If you click on the link

Ver detalles

You get seller information:

Información detallada sobre el vendedor
Vendedor comercial

Nombre de empresa: Paper Cavalier Ltd.

Tipo de empresa: Empresa privada

Número de registro mercantil: 05879764

Número de IVA: GB101519167

Número de teléfono: +442080640889

Dirección de servicio al cliente:

Block K, Unit 104

100 Clements Road

London

SE16 4DG

GB

Dirección empresarial:

100 Clements Road

Block K, Unit 104

London

London

SE16 4DG

GB

There is one more option for "trusted sellers" in the drop-down:

BEANNY

Of you click this link you get:

Información detallada sobre el vendedor
Vendedor comercial

Nombre de empresa: Lee Bing Fung

Tipo de empresa: Empresa privada

Número de registro mercantil: TN23971294

Dirección empresarial:

173 MILLVIEW SQ SW

Calgary

AB

T2Y 3Y5

CA

The hardcover version "cancelled" by Ingram abt two years ago has ISBN 978-2919787586, one of our numbers from the Luxembourg National ISBN Number provider.

It appears that the trick to "whitewash" counterfeit newly printed copies is to call them "second hand, good condition" meaning the books were never opened, they are newly printed using the pdf files uploaded to Ingram?

Another trick appears to be to call the books "collector´s items"?

On ebay you have independent small sellers but here the "trusted sellers" are integrated into Amazon´s main page.

You enter via "SonicBW" as shown in the search bar, but the displayed 100,000 books are from the general Amazon library. If you select "author" the algorithm selects a number of titles which are different between the "trusted sellers" so as not to be conspicuous.

If you search amazon.com author+title specific you also get correct information (4 Apr 2023)

RESULTS

Cats in Art Timeline

by Cristina Berna | Dec 15, 2022

5.0*5.0 out of 5 stars* (1)

Paperback

$84.92 $84.92

Delivery **Fri, Apr 21**

Or fastest delivery **Thu, Apr 13**

Ships to Austria

Cats in Art: Artists A - Z

by Cristina Berna and Eric Thomsen | Nov 18, 2019

No reviews

Paperback

$79.95 $79.95

$10.04 delivery

Ships to Austria

Temporarily out of stock.

https://www.amazon.com/s?k=cristina+berna+cats+in+art&i=stripbooks-intl-ship&crid=1275L2IZ540C3&sprefix=cristina+berna+cats+in+art%2Cstripbooks-intl-ship%2C268&ref=nb_sb_noss

Now take our ninth book uploaded via our agent in Sevilla

Hiroshige 100 Famous Views of Edo

Cristina Berna Precio 99.95€ ISBN 9781956773958

This is another of our books which received high ratings, five stars out of five, when it was first published via Ingram, which we were very proud of - so, why would Ingram cancel this book???

What is it in this book that is besmirching Ingram´s catalogue???

No, there has to be another reason?

This book was uploaded 16 Dec 2022 to our agent.

According to our agent this book has a book page with amazon.es

Enlaces

Plataforma	Enlace
ama	https://www.amazon.es/s/ref=nb_sb_noss?__mk_es_ES=%C3%85M%C3%85%C5%BD%C3%95%C3%91&url=search-alias%3Daps&field-keywords=9781956773958

If you click the link, you get the following information

Utilice menos palabras clave o pruebe con estas
No hay resultados para 9781956773958.

El precio y otros detalles pueden variar en función del tamaño y el color del producto.

This is clearly wrong, and a systematic "error" shown previously, designed to, we feel, maliciously suppress the sale of our books in coordination and cooperation with Ingram?

If you do the SPECIFIC search in amazon.com, 'meaning you combine title and author, Amazon pushes OTHER authors instead of showing our book.

Amazon is hijacking the interest in our five-star book to push other books.

Amazon is creaming off interest in our book to hurt our sales and income.

RESULTS

[Hiroshige. One Hundred Famous Views of Edo]

by Lorenz Bichler and Melanie Trede | Aug 26, 2010

4.8*4.8 out of 5 stars* (814)

Hardcover

Calendar

Hiroshige: One Hundred Famous Views of Edo
4.1*4.1 out of 5 stars* (4)

Hardcover

$18.45$18.45

Only 1 left in stock - order soon.

More Buying Choices
$9.64(11 used & new offers)

Hiroshige: One Hundred Famous Views of Edo

by Henry D. Smith and Ando Hiroshige | Apr 17, 2000

4.9*4.9 out of 5 stars* (20)

Hardcover

Paperback

Hiroshige: 100 Famous Views of Edo

No reviews

Hardcover

$12.95 $12.95

$12.36 delivery

Ships to Austria

Temporarily out of stock.

Paperback

$79.95 $79.95

$10.47 delivery

Ships to Austria

Usually ships within 2 to 3 days.

More Buying Choices
$79.72(4 new offers)

Yoshitaki Kunikazu Nansuitei Yoshiyuki 100 Views of Osaka: Hardcover

by Cristina Berna and Eric Thomsen | Nov 23, 2020

5.0*5.0 out of 5 stars* (1)

Hardcover

Paperback

$106.19 $106.19

Delivery **Thu, Apr 20**

Or fastest delivery **Thu, Apr 13**

Ships to Austria

Use fewer keywords or try these instead

The link is

https://www.amazon.com/s?k=cristina+berna+hiroshige+100+famous+views+of+edo&i=stripbooks-intl-ship&crid=3MCKG87WBBXI8&sprefix=cristina+berna+hiroshige+100+famous+views+of+edo%2Cstripbooks-intl-ship%2C232&ref=nb_sb_noss

We allege Amazon.com is using predatory practices to suppress the sales of our five-star books in cooperation with Ingram, which "cancelled" this book even though it sold well and got a fine review and was approved in writing by Ingram?

We allege this is fraud, fraud on us, fraud on the customers and fraud on the European Union competition policy.

A distant lead to us as authors in in the version in black and white sold via another printer, which we used in an attempt to test this channel

Top of Form

Buy new:

$79.95

You Earn: 160 pts Learn more

No Import Fees Deposit & $10.47 Shipping to Austria Details

$10.47 delivery

Deliver to Eric - 5020 Salzburg 5020

Usually ships within 2 to 3 days

Qty:

1 Qty:1

Add to Cart

Submit Buy Now

Payment

Secure transaction

Ships from

Amazon.com

Sold by

Amazon.com

Payment

Secure transaction

We work hard to protect your security and privacy. Our payment security system encrypts your information during transmission. We don't share your credit card details with third-party sellers, and we don't sell your information to others. Learn more

Ships from

Amazon.com

Sold by

Amazon.com

Return policy: Eligible for Return, Refund or Replacement within 30 days of receipt

Add a gift receipt for easy returns

Add to List Add to List

Have one to sell?

Sell on Amazon

Submit Add to book club

Not in a club? Learn more

Sponsored

Hiroshige
100 Famous
Views of
Edo
Cristina Berna
Eric Thomsen

Hiroshige 100 Famous Views Of Edo Paperback – May 8, 2019

by Cristina Berna (Author)

No reviews

See all formats and editions

- Hardcover
  $12.95
  You Earn: 26 pts
  1 New from $12.95

- Paperback
  $79.95
  You Earn: 160 pts
  4 New from $79.72

and you only get the author name if you click as fifth click on this version,

and how many potential customers go to the fifth click????

If you click the link to "new" you get a drop down to the Amazon book depository in the UK, confusingly also claiming to be in the US.

But this does not take away that Amazon is pushing three other authors and hiding the author name Cristina Berna deep deep down in the fifth click on the fourth book result......

This is predatory, we feel.

Granted there is a sixth result, and this is for one of our books:

Blick ins Buch ↓

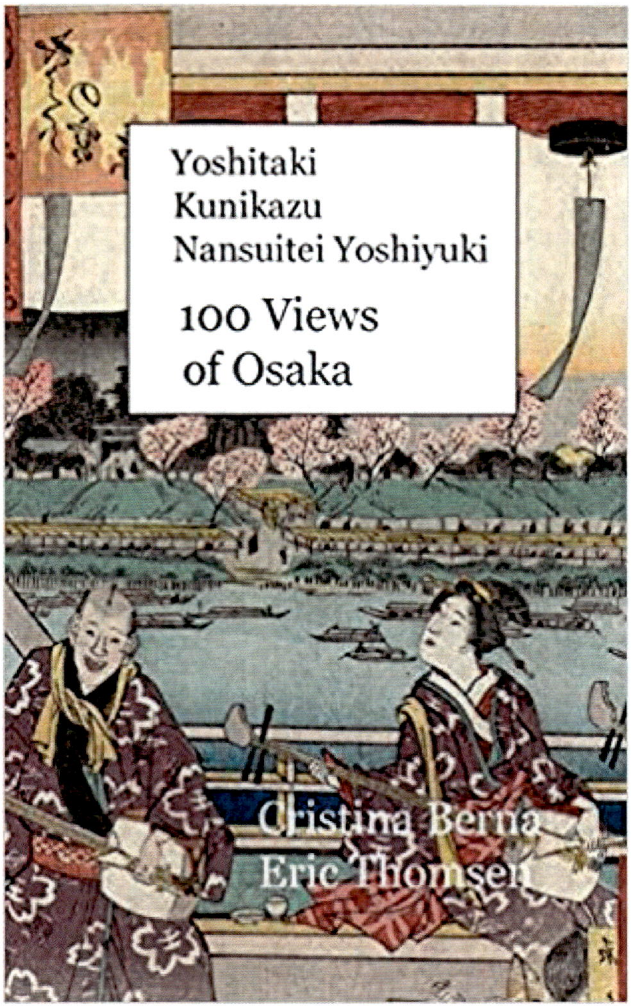

Yoshitaki Kunikazu Nansuitei Yoshiyuki 100

Views of Osaka: Hardcover Hardcover – 23 Nov. 2020

English edition by Cristina Berna (Autor), Eric Thomsen (Autor)

*5.0 out of 5 stars_* 1 rating

See all formats and editions

- **Hardcover**
  €165.40
  Other new and used from €146.13

- Paperback
  €102.75
  Other new from €99.95

Product details

- **Publisher** : Missys Clan (23 Nov. 2020)
- **Language** : English
- **Hardcover** : 258 pages
- **ISBN-10** : 164945452X
- **ISBN-13** : 978-1649454522
- **Dimensions** : 15.19 x 2.06 x 22.91 cm
- **Customer reviews:**
  *5.0 out of 5 stars_* 1 rating

This is another of our five-star-out-of-five books, but you know what?

Amazon leads you to the counterfeit hardcover version issued 23 Nov 2020.

Take now the ninth book we uploaded to our agent in Sevilla, another of our books which got a great review in the Ingram version with five stars, and a book Ingram has "cancelled" purely as a financial punishment without lawful basis after approving it in writing - to punish us for -

yes, for what?

Having political and religious beliefs their private censors don´t like and which they unlawfully enforce especially on the European Union?

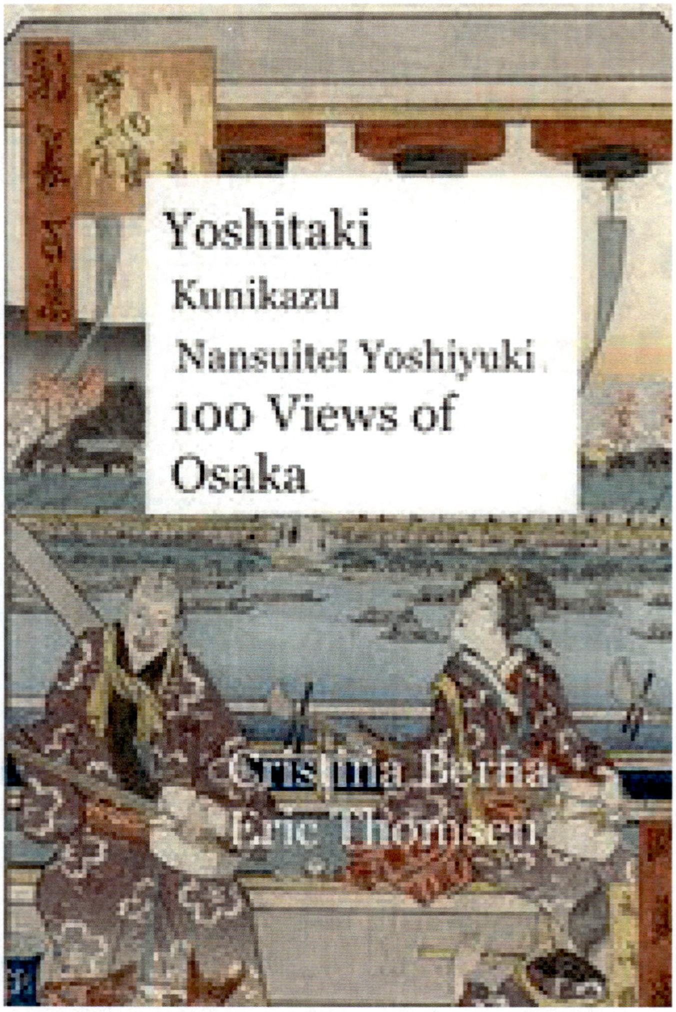

Yoshitaki Kunikazu Nansuitei Yoshiyuki 100 Views of Osaka

Cristina Berna Precio 99.95€ ISBN 978-1-956773-96-5

This book was uploaded to our agent 16 Dec 2022.

It has a link to a book page in Amazon.es according to our agent:

Enlaces

Plataforma	Enlace
ama	https://www.amazon.es/s/ref=nb_sb_noss?__mk_es_ES=%C3%85M%C3%85%C5%BD%C3%95%C3%91&url=search-alias%3Daps&field-keywords=9781956773965

If you click this link you get the following result

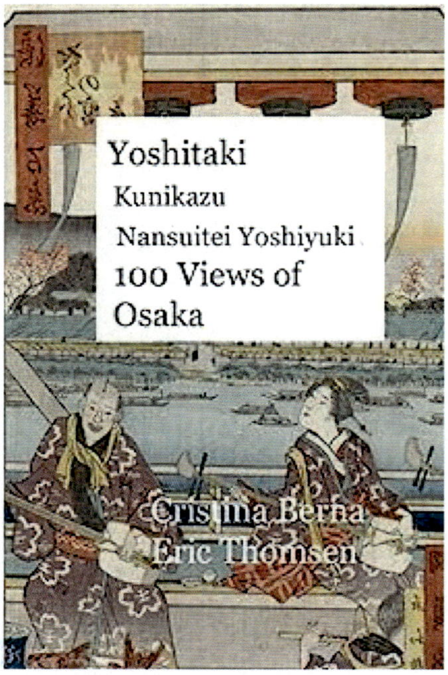

Yoshitaki Kunikazu Nansuitei Yoshiyuki 100 Views of Osaka

Edición en Inglés
de Cristina Berna

5.0*5,0 de 5 estrellas* (1)

Tapa blanda

99,95 € 99,95€

Entrega por 5,73 € el **ju., 6 de abr.**

Entrega más rápida el **mi., 5 de abr.**

Otro formato: Tapa dura

This is half correct information.

It has a link to hard cover, tapa dura....

and tapa dura is only available as counterfeit copy of the original version in Ingram – or Ingram has allowed without permission, in the context to defraud the copyright holders, Amazon to use the pdf files the copyright holders uploaded to Ingram for the purpose of World Wide distribution as promised by Ingram – of course subject to Ingram reporting sales by the end of each month and paying author´s fees 90 days later?

If you click the tapa dura link you get this result

Nuevo:

90,78 €

Precio recomendado: 133,48 €

Ahorra: 42,70 € (32 %)

Los precios incluyen IVA. El precio final a pagar al finalizar la compra puede variar según la dirección de entrega. Ver detalles

Entrega por 5,86 € el **jueves, 6 de abril**. Haz el pedido en 12 horas 56 mins. Ver detalles

Enviar a Austria

Sólo queda(n) 1 en stock

Añadir a la cesta Añadir a la cesta

Submit Comprar ya

Transacción segura

Envío desde

Amazon

Vendido por

Amazon

Devoluciones

Se puede devolver en un plazo de 30 días a partir de la fecha de recepción

Envío desde

Amazon

Vendido por

Amazon

Devoluciones

Se puede devolver en un plazo de 30 días a partir de la fecha de recepción

El producto se puede devolver en su condición original para obtener un reembolso completo o un reemplazo en un plazo de 30 días a partir de la fecha de recepción

Leer la política de devoluciones completa

☐ Añade un ticket de regalo para facilitar las devoluciones

Patrocinado

¿Tienes uno para vender?

Vender en Amazon

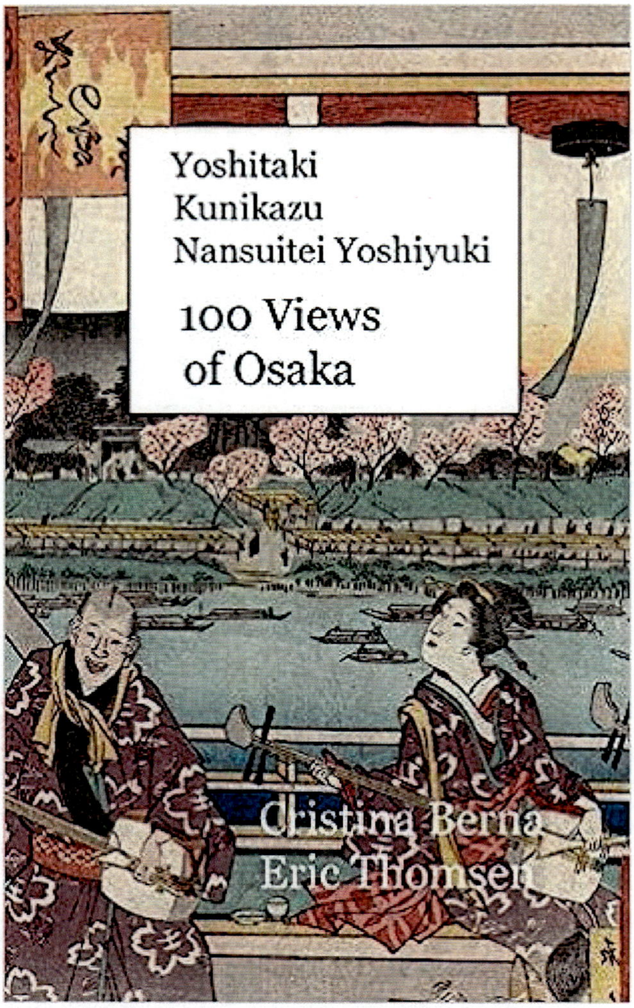

Yoshitaki Kunikazu Nansuitei Yoshiyuki 100 Views of Osaka:

Hardcover Tapa dura – 23 noviembre 2020

Edición en Inglés de Cristina Berna (Autor), Eric Thomsen (Autor)

5,0 de 5 estrellas 1 valoración

Ver todos los formatos y ediciones

- Tapa dura
  90,78 €
  Otros nuevo a partir de 90,78 €

- Tapa blanda
  99,95 €
  Otros nuevo a partir de 99,95 €

Viewing Osaka through the series 100 Views of Naniwa (Osaka) is an amazing experience. It is a well executed repetition over a format by Hiroshige. Some add a "Famous" to the title.

This series is by three artists, Utagawa Yoshitaki, Utagawa Kunikazu and Nansuitei Yoshiyuki.

Hiroshige I created his revolutionary series 100 Famous Views of Edo over three years, 1856-1859.

This led to the publishing of copy series 100 Views of Naniwa (Osaka) by other artists. The book here is based mainly on prints in the Museum of Fine Arts in Boston and Osaka Municipal Museum collections.

Hiroshige I had done his own series *Famous Views of Naniwa* (Osaka), 10 prints, as early as 1834, but it was his *100 Famous Views of Edo* that caused the significant copy production.

Copying ideas and prints was quite normal in the Edo Period Japan print business.

Utagawa Yoshitaki

Utagawa Yoshitaki (歌川 芳滝, April 13, 1841 - June 28, 1899), was is also known as Ichiyōsai Yoshitaki (一養斎 芳滝). Yoshitaki was a Japanese designer of ukiyo-e woodblock prints who was active in both Edo (Tokyo) and Osaka. He was also a painter and newspaper illustrator. His father was a paste merchant, and Yoshitaki became a student of Utagawa Yoshiume (1819-1879). Yoshitaki was the most prolific designer of woodblock prints in Osaka from the 1860s to the 1880s, producing more than 1,200 different prints, almost all of kabuki actors. Judging from archives of sold prints since 2001, most of Kunikazu's output were actor and kabuki theater subjects. But he also made a few landscape series. One is titled Hundred Views of Naniwa - Naniwa Hyakkei published by Wataki. Naniwa is another name for Osaka. After the success of Hiroshige Ando (Hiroshige I) in the landscape genre, these Views of ... series had gained some popularity among the Japanese print buying public.

His earliest prints were published when he had barely entered his teens. In 1855 he left Yoshiume to be an independent artist. For a period of twenty years, Yoshitaki was the most prolific of Osaka print artists, producing more than 1,200 designs, nearly all yakusha-e (actor pictures.) In addition to creating woodblock prints of actors and of landscapes1, Yoshitaki, using the artist names Sasaki Yoshitaki 笹木芳瀧 (starting in 1875) and Nakai Yoshitaki 中井芳瀧, created (wrote and illustrated) specialized woodblock prints called nishki-e shinbun for several Osaka newspapers including the Osaka nishikiga shinbun, Osaka nishikie shinwa, Kanzen choaku nishikiga shinbun, and Shinbun zue. Yoshitaki also remained active as a painter, exhibiting both in Japan and internationally, winning bronze medals at the first two Naikoku Kaiga Kyoshin Kai (National Paintings Fair) in 1882 and 1884 and a meritorious mention at the fourth Naikoku Kangyo Hakurankai (National Expo for the Promotion of Industry.) As with many woodblock artists he also worked as a commerical artist, creating theater billboards and illustrations for a sake company.In 1880, he moved to Kyoto and in 1885 he moved to Sakai where he died in 1889. He is buried at Nanshuji on Ryukozan in Sakai.

Product details

- **Publisher** : Missys Clan (23 Nov. 2020)
- **Language** : English
- **Hardcover** : 258 pages
- **ISBN-10** : 164945452X
- **ISBN-13** : 978-1649454522
- **Dimensions** : 15.19 x 2.06 x 22.91 cm
-
- **Customer reviews:**
  *5.0 out of 5 stars_* 1 rating

If you click on the hard cover there is a drop down stating the seller of this counterfeit version is Amazon itself, Amazon is allegedly selling our books as pirate copy, unless of course Amazon can show an invoice, and Amazon has not been willing to show us such invoices.

In other words – Amazon is placing a link to the counterfeit version of the book they are selling – introducing it into the book page for the legal paperback version we are selling.

Amazon is not offering sales data or to pay author´s fees.

The counterfeit version isn´t cheap – this means Jeff Bezos we feel is telling us he is certain he can misappropriate from us with impunity. We feel he says we don´t dare to object because then he will close the channel completely to us like Ingram did, for no good reason. As revenge? This is private taxation without legal basis.

If you click on the link in the counterfeit hardcover version page

- Other new and used from €146.13

You get the following offers in a drop-down without a link

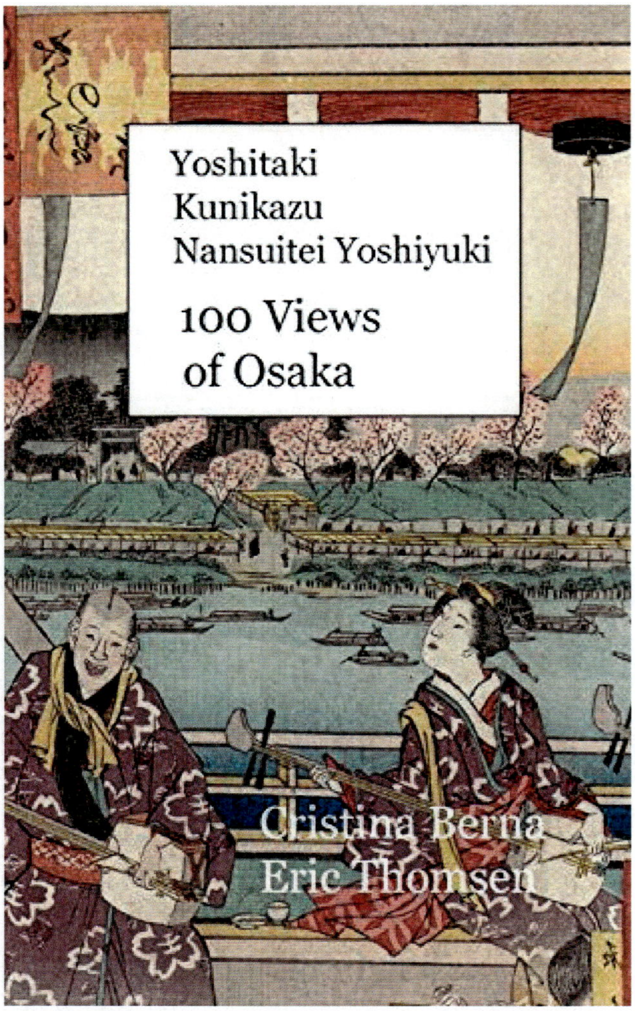

Yoshitaki Kunikazu Nansuitei Yoshiyuki 100 Views of Osaka: Hardcover
Hardcover

1 rating

New

€165.40 €165.40

FREE delivery **Thursday, April 13**

Submit Add to Basket

Dispatches from

Amazon

Sold by

Amazon

Return policy

See less

Used - Like New

€146.13 €146.13

FREE delivery **May 4 - 26**. Details

Submit Add to Basket

Dispatches from

BB Corps UK

Sold by

BB Corps UK

(780 ratings)

70% positive over last 12 months

Return policy

Amazon offers

New
€165.40

The trivial question – where does Amazon get this book from

Another of Amazon´s "trusted sellers" BB Corps UK offers this book as

Used - Like New
€146.13 €146.13

We believe this book was newly printed, was never sold, was never used – but that is up to an investigation. BB Corps UK is innocent until proven guilty, as Nancy Pelosi says. In Manhattan.

If you click on the link to BB Corps UK you get this information:

Detailed Seller Information
Business seller

Business Name: BB Corps

Business Type: Privately-owned business

Trade Register Number: 808499107

VAT Number: FR14808499107

Phone number: 0033768326547

Customer Services Address:

1 rue des mobiles

Lyon

69003

FR

Business Address:

1

rue des mobiles

Lyon

69003

FR

Link:

https://www.amazon.de/sp?language=en&ie=UTF8&seller=A1J52ABXQUH3J8&isAmazo

nFulfilled=0&asin=164945452X&ref_=olp_
merch_name_1

So, BB Corps UK is NOT in the UK – it is a French firm. Deceptive, as the reviewer wrote?

Why would you give the customer the impression it is a UK business, when it is a French business?

BB Corps UK also has a “storefront” within the Amazon world:

Link:

https://www.amazon.de/s?me=A1J52ABXQ
UH3J8&language=en&marketplaceID=A1PA
6795UKMFR9

BB Corps UK has purchased a lesser plan than the others we have seen – it has

1-16 of over 50,000 results

If you search the author "Cristina Berna" on BB Corps UK`s storefront, you get this result:

4 results for **"cristina berna"**

Sort by: Featured Sort by:Featured

RESULTS

Learn about these results.

Joaquín Sorolla Portraits 3: Hardcover

English edition | by Cristina Berna and Eric Thomsen

1.0*1.0 out of 5 stars* (1)

Hardcover

Yoshitaki Kunikazu Nansuitei Yoshiyuki 100 Views of Osaka: Hardcover

English edition | by Cristina Berna and Eric Thomsen

5.0*5.0 out of 5 stars* (1)

Hardcover

Hiroshige 53 Stations of the Tōkaidō Jinbutso

English edition | by Cristina Berna and Eric Thomsen

2.0*2.0 out of 5 stars* (5)

Paperback

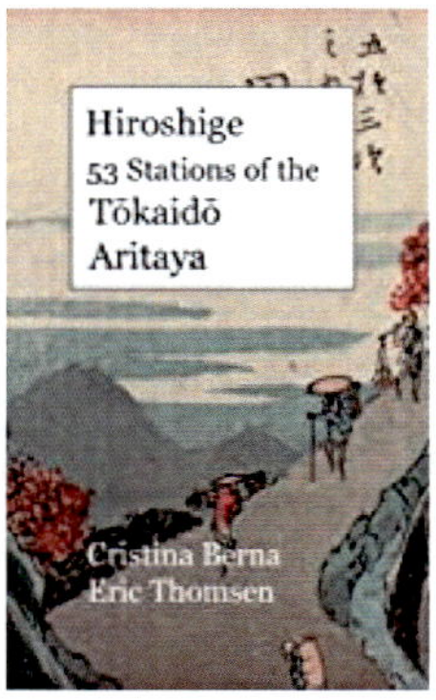

Hiroshige 53 Stations of the Tōkaidō Aritaya: Premium

English edition | by Cristina Berna and Eric Thomsen

No reviews

Hardcover

DO YOU NEED HELP?

Visit the help section or contact us

We won´t go through them all now, but suffice to say – these appear all to be counterfeit versions of our books. Ingram “cancelled” them abt two years ago – all of them! After having approved them in writing – and has given no good reason for doing so.

Let us go to our 11th book uploaded with our agent:

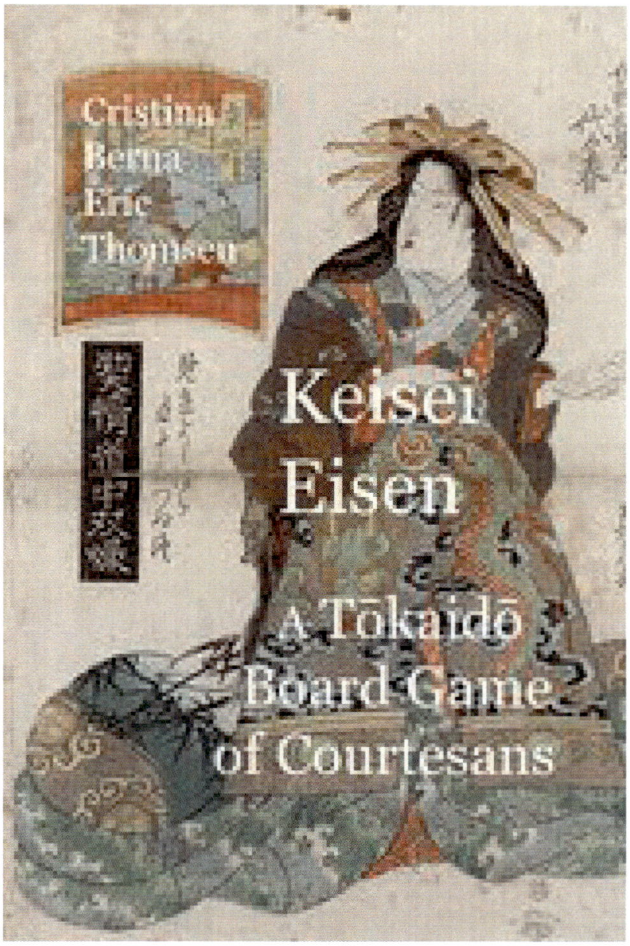

Keisai EisenA Tōkaidō Board Game of Courtesans

Cristina Berna Precio 149.95€ ISBN 978-1-956773-92-7

This book was uploaded to our agent 19 Dec 2022.

It has a link, according to our agent, to a book page in Amazon

Enlaces

Plataforma	Enlace
am	https://www.amazon.es/s/ref=nb_sb_noss?__mk_es_ES=%C3%85M%C3%85%C5%BD%C3%95%C3%91&url=search-alias%3Daps&field-keywords=9781956773927

If you click on this link you get the following information

Keisai Eisen A Tōkaidō Board Game of Courtesans: Fifty-three Pairings in the Yoshiwara

Edición en Inglés

de Cristina Berna

Sin reseñas

Tapa blanda

149,95€ 149,95€

Entrega por 5,78 € el **mi., 12 de abr.**

There are no links to "hardcopy" or counterfeit versions "cancelled" by Ingram.....simply because this book was never on Ingram and was not cancelled.

We can do a search author+title specific on amazon.com

You get the following result:

Use fewer keywords or try these instead
No results for cristina berne keisai eisen a tokaido board game 53 pairings in the yoshiwara

https://www.amazon.de/-/en/s?k=cristina+berne+keisai+eisen+a+tokaido+board+game+53+pairings+in+the+yoshiwara&dm=true&crid=2JTD09GA6USPO&sprefix=cristina+berne+keisai+eisen+a+tokaido+board+game+53+pairings+in+the+yoshiwara%2Caps%2C111&ref=sr_moz_back

You can speculate – but if you want a conspiracy theory – Amazon is punishing us for not having a previous version in Ingram they can copy and sell as counterfeit?

It does not help to remove the author name...

But if the book has an Amazon book page, why is the result not coming up when you search it on the general site??

The book is about a somewhat difficult but very talented Japanese ukiyo-e artist Keisai Eisen, who is fantastic in his rendering – in woodblock print – of clothing and cloth patterns...

He did part of the "69 Stations of the Nakasendo" but due to too much wine and women the publisher let Hiroshige finish the series. We have published this series as well. Keisai Eisen by the way at one time also ran a brothel. It explains the faces of some of his beauties.

Let us go to book no 12 we have uploaded to our agent:

Hokusai 36 Views of Mount Fuji

Cristina Berna Precio 99.95€ ISBN 978-1-956773-98-9

This book was uploaded to our agent 19 Dec 2022. It was actually the first book we did on Japanese prints. It was first on Amazon then on Ingram since 2017. We did it in several variations and sizes. It sold well.

The book has a link to a book page in Amazon, according to our agent:

Enlaces

Plataforma	**Enlace**
am	https://www.amazon.es/s/ref=nb_sb_noss?__mk_es_ES=%C3%85M%C3%85%C5%BD%C3%95%C3%91&url=search-alias%3Daps&field-keywords=9781956773989

If you click this link, you get the following result:

Hokusai 36 Views of Mount Fuji….
Edición en Inglés
de Cristina Berna

Sin reseñas

Tapa blanda

99,95€ 99,95€

Entrega por 5,71 € el **ju., 13 de abr.**

If you click on ”tapa blanda” you are shunted into Amazon general to this link:

https://www.amazon.es/Hokusai-36-Views-Mount-Fuji/dp/1956773983/ref=sr_1_1?__mk_es_ES=%C3%85M%C3%85%C5%BD%C3%95%C3%91&keywords=9781956773989&qid=1680878900&sr=8-1

You have the following information:

Hokusai
36 Views of
Mount Fuji
Cristina Berna
Eric Thomsen

Hokusai 36 Views of Mount Fuji... Tapa blanda – 19 diciembre 2022

Edición en Inglés de Cristina Berna (Autor)

Sin reseñas

Ver todos los formatos y ediciones

- **Tapa blanda**
  99,95 €
  Otros nuevo a partir de 99,95 €

Detalles del producto

- **Editorial** : VESTERNAES (19 diciembre 2022)
- **Idioma** : Inglés
- **Tapa blanda** : 218 páginas
- **ISBN-10** : 1956773983
- **ISBN-13** : 978-1956773989
- **Peso del producto** : 345 g
- **Dimensiones** : 14 x 1.27 x 21 cm

Click on the link Otros nuevo a partir de 99,95 € to get the following offer:

Hokusai 36 Views of Mount Fuji…..
Tapa blanda

Nuevo
99,95 €99,95€

Entrega por 5,71 € el **jueves, 13 de abril**. Ver detalles

Submit Añadir a la cesta

Envía por

Amazon

Vendedor

Amazon

Ver menos

Amazon is offering this book as

Nuevo

99,95€ 99,95€

Amazon is offering the book as new and at list price.

Everything is fine.....

Click then on Ver todos los formatos y ediciones and you get the following result:

1 formatos y ediciones¿Cómo se ordenan los resultados?

- **Tapa blanda (1)**

Hokusai 36 Views of Mount Fuji.....

99,95 €€99,95
Nuevo desde 99,95 €

Calificación	(0)
ISBN-13	978-1956773989

If you do a general search on Amazon author+title specific, you get the following result as the *second* book on the list:

Hokusai 36 Views of Mt Fuji

English edition | by Cristina Berna and Eric Thomsen | 28 Jan 2019

No reviews

Paperback

Currently unavailable.

The link to the search (7 Apr 2023) is

https://www.amazon.de/s?k=cristina+berna+36+views+of+mt+fuji&crid=2FASSHFBN4NS3&sprefix=cristina+berna+36+views+of+mt+fuji%2Caps%2C127&ref=nb_sb_noss_2

There is *no* link to the book we uploaded 19 Dec 2022 via our agent to Amazon.

Again, if you want a conspiracy theory – this is because Amazon is punishing us financially by blocking the book from being searchable?

If you do a general search just for "36 Views of Mt Fuji" you get a lot of other authors and books, but you also get this one of ours:

Hokusai 36 Views of Mt Fuji: Large format

English edition | by Cristina Berna and Eric Thomsen | 31 Jan 2019

No reviews

Paperback

Currently unavailable.

The link to this general search (7 Apr 2023) is:

https://www.amazon.de/s?k=36+views+of+mt+fuji&crid=3DBQ61N32JPNM&sprefix=36+views+of+mt+fuji%2Caps%2C145&ref=nb_sb_noss_2

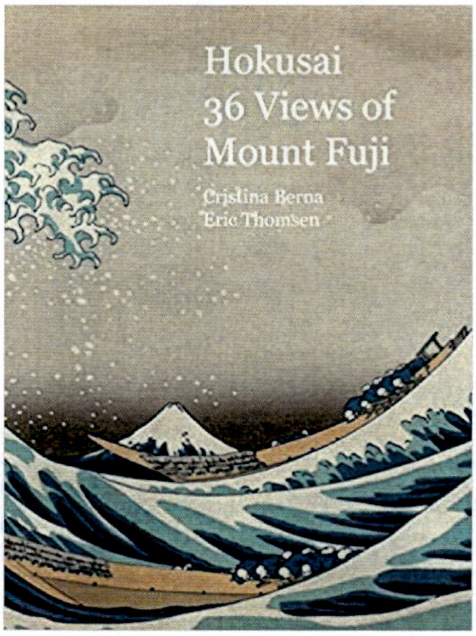

Hokusai 36 Views of Mt Fuji: Large format Paperback – Illustrated, 31 Jan. 2019

English edition by Cristina Berna (Autor), Eric Thomsen (Autor)

No reviews

See all formats and editions

- **Paperback**
  —

Product details

- **Publisher** : Missys Clan; Illustrated edition (31 Jan. 2019)
- **Language** : English
- **Paperback** : 156 pages
- **ISBN-10** : 291978708X
- **ISBN-13** : 978-2919787081
- **Dimensions** : 20.96 x 1.07 x 27.94 cm

This was done I large format so that customers wanting large pictures could get that – see reviews above.

But Ingram "cancelled" this book together with 290 other titles for no known good reason, abt two years ago.

Amazon clutters the search with a book that is not available instead of the one which is available – why?

If you just for the sake of it click on "Cristina Berna" (author), you get this result:

Hiroshige Famous Places of Naniwa (Osaka)

English edition | by Cristina Berna and Eric Thomsen | 9 Jun 2020

5.0*5.0 out of 5 stars* (1)

Paperback

€41.93 €41.93

Get it **Thursday, 13 Apr**

FREE Delivery by Amazon

Only 1 left in stock.

More buying choices
€32.28 (2 new offers)

Hardcover

€43.10 €43.10

Get it **Wednesday, 26 Apr - Friday, 19 May**

€5.75 delivery

Only 3 left in stock.

More b uying choices
€41.92 (2 new offers)

Apparently a counterfeit book in two versions – and that is ALL Amazon is showing for this productive writer.

Say again this is a "conspiracy theory"....

Go now to the 13th book we uploaded to our agent:

Hiroshige Kunisada Kuniyoshi 53 Pairings of the Tōkaidō

Cristina Berna Precio 99.95€ ISBN 978-1-956773-97-2

This book was uploaded to our agent 28 Dec 2022.

It has a link to an Amazon book page according to our agent:

Enlaces

Plataforma	Enlace
am	https://www.amazon.es/s/ref=nb_sb_noss?__mk_es_ES=%C3%85M%C3%85%C5%BD%C3%95%C3%91&url=search-alias%3Daps&field-keywords=9781956773972

If you click this link you get the following result:

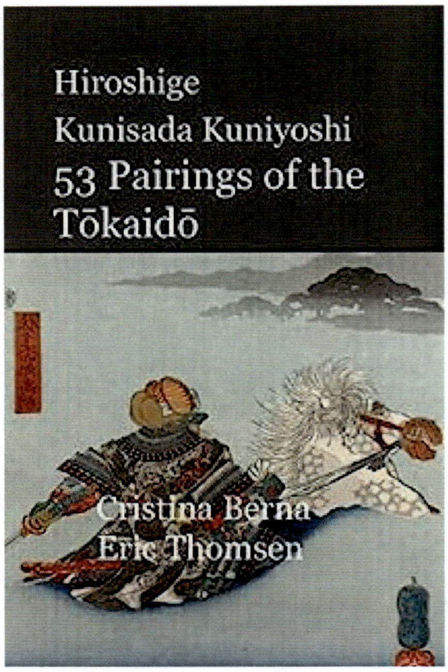

Hiroshige Kunisada Kuniyoshi 53 Pairings of the Tōkaidō

Edición en Inglés
de Cristina Berna

3,0*3,0 de 5 estrellas* (1)

Tapa blanda

99,95€ 99,95€

Entrega por 5,79 € el **mi., 12 de abr.**

Otro formato: Tapa dura

Note again how Amazon is filtering in a link to the alleged counterfeit versions they sell into the page for the legal version.

Click on the link to "Tapa dura" – hardcover – and you get the following result:

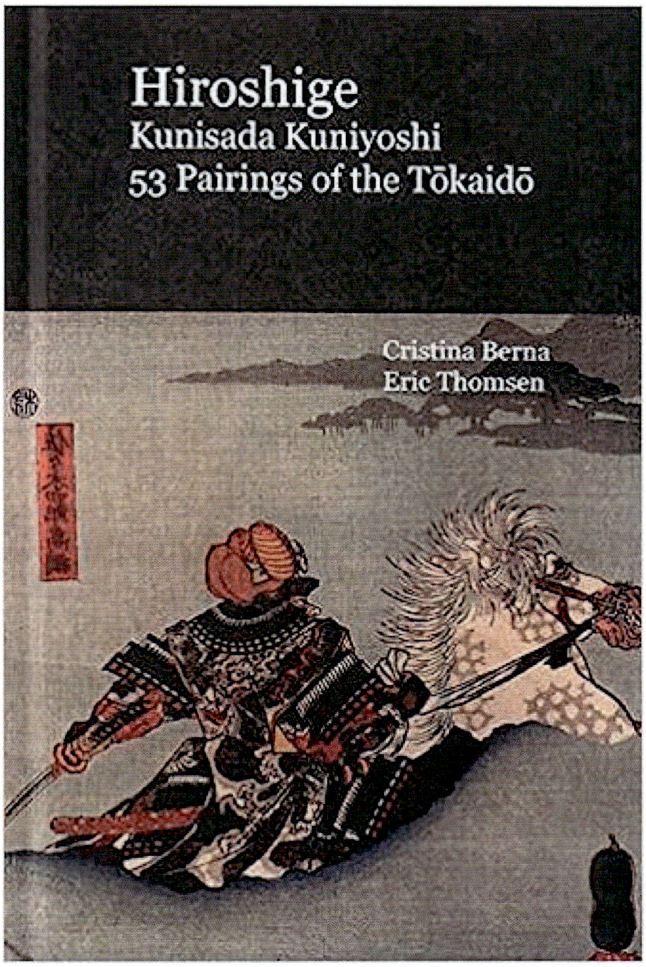

Hiroshige Kunisada Kuniyoshi 53 Pairings of the Tōkaidō: Hardcover Tapa dura – 16 diciembre 2020

Edición en Inglés de Cristina Berna (Autor), Eric Thomsen (Autor)

3,0 de 5 estrellas 1 valoración

Ver todos los formatos y ediciones

- **Tapa dura**
  desde 46,40 €
  Otros nuevo y de 2ª mano a partir de 46,40 €

- Tapa blanda
  99,95 €
  Otros nuevo a partir de 99,95 €

Detalles del producto

- **Editorial** : Missys Clan (16 diciembre 2020)
- **Idioma** : Inglés
- **Tapa dura** : 328 páginas

- **ISBN-10** : 1637526717
- **ISBN-13** : 978-1637526712
- **Peso del producto** : 762 g
- **Dimensiones** : 15.24 x 2.69 x 22.86 cm
- **Opiniones de los clientes:**
  3,0 de 5 estrellas 1 valoración

This hardcover version has three stars out of five. No review.

There is a link to the counterfeit versions in hardback

Otros nuevo y de 2ª mano a partir de 46,40 €

If you click on it, you get the following information in a drop-down without a link

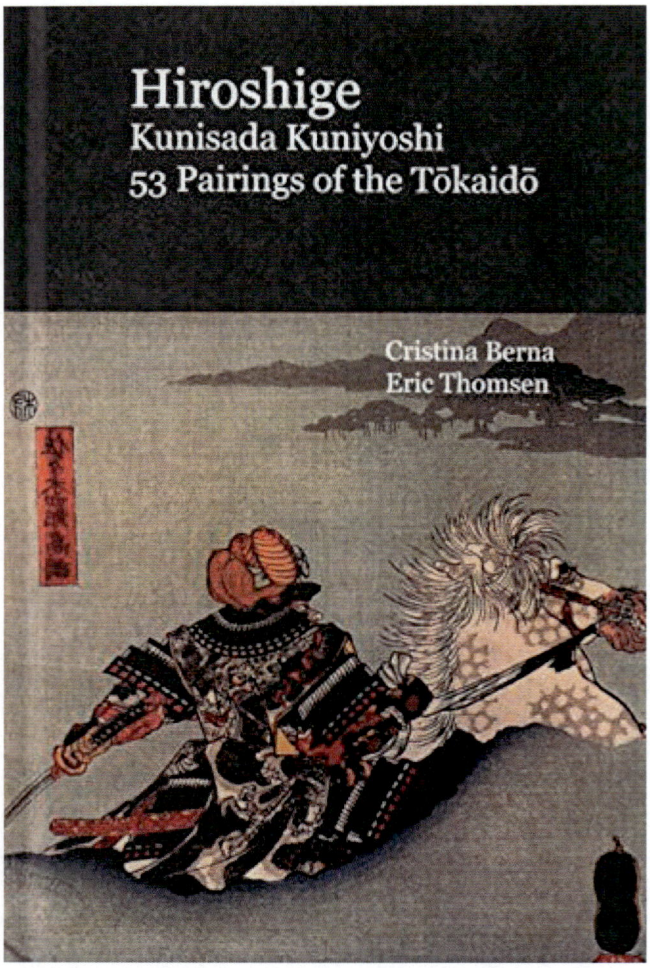

Hiroshige Kunisada Kuniyoshi 53 Pairings of the Tōkaidō: Hardcover
Tapa dura

1 valoración

1 opción
ordenado por precio + envío: de menor a mayor

Filtrar (4)

De 2ª mano - Como nuevo

De 2ª mano - Muy bueno

+2

Borrar todo

De 2ª mano - Como nuevo
46,40 €46,40€

Entrega por 5,96 € entre el **10 - 31 de mayo**. Ver detalles

Submit Añadir a la cesta

Envía por

DMI Media Europe

Vendedor

DMI Media Europe

(50 calificaciones)
69 % positivas en los últimos 12 meses

You get the offer of a second hand book as "good as new"

De 2ª mano - Como nuevo
46,40€ 46,40€

The offer is from

DMI Media Europe

If you open the link you get this information:

Tipo de empresa: Empresa privada
Número de registro mercantil: 81-4265234
Dirección de servicio al cliente:
Moncreiffe Business Centre Friarton Road
Suite B1
Perth
PH2 8DG
GB
Dirección empresarial:
SUITE24-1013
6271 SAINT AUGUSTINE RD
Jacksonville
Florida
32217-2523
US

DMI Media is a business with offices in Perth, UK and St Augustine, Florida..

https://www.amazon.es/sp?ie=UTF8&seller=A1894GFVA6IFD7&isAmazonFulfilled=0&asin=1637526717&ref_=olp_merch_name_1

The business has a storefront inside the Amazon book world:

Visita Escaparate de DMI Media Europe

If you click on that you get

1-16 de más de 200.000 resultados

https://www.amazon.es/s?me=A1894GFVA6IFD7&marketplaceID=A1RKKUPIHCS9HS

DMI Media Europe offers 200,000 book titles on Amazon.....all of them appears to be second-hand....????

If you search the author on DMI Media Europe inside the Amazon book world, you get

Resultados

Más información sobre estos resultados.

Joaquín Sorolla Nudes

Edición en Inglés | de Cristina Berna

1,4*1,4 de 5 estrellas* (3)

Tapa blanda

Hokusai 53 Stations of the Tōkaidō 1801

Edición en Inglés | de Cristina Berna y Eric Thomsen

3,0*3,0 de 5 estrellas* (1)

Tapa blanda

Joaquín Sorolla Portraits 3: Hardcover

Edición en Inglés | de Cristina Berna y Eric Thomsen

1,0*1,0 de 5 estrellas* (1)

Tapa dura

Eleanor of Aquitaine

Edición en Inglés | de Cristina Berna

Sin reseñas

Tapa blanda

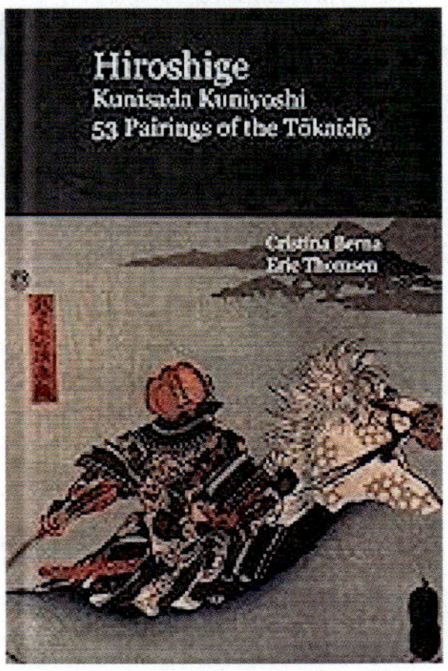

Hiroshige Kunisada Kuniyoshi 53 Pairings of the Tōkaidō: Hardcover

Edición en Inglés | de Cristina Berna y Eric Thomsen

3,0*3,0 de 5 estrellas* (1)

Tapa dura

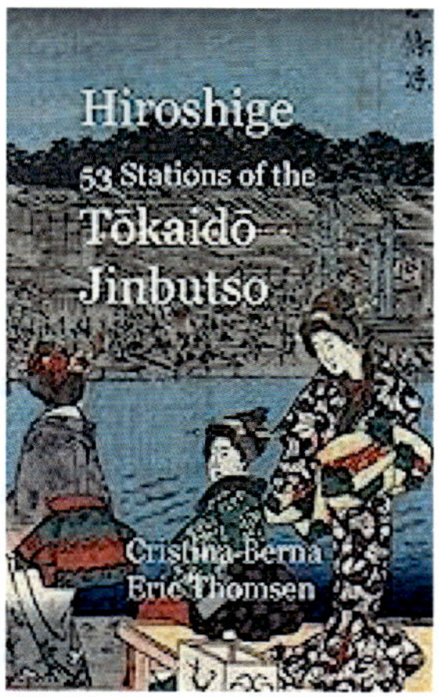

Hiroshige 53 Stations of the Tōkaidō Jinbutso: Premium

Edición en Inglés | de Cristina Berna y Eric Thomsen

Sin reseñas

Tapa dura

Hiroshige 53 Stations of the Tōkaidō Aritaya

Edición en Inglés | de Cristina Berna y Eric Thomsen

Sin reseñas

Tapa blanda

Tōkaidō Meisho Zue Vol 3 Rito Akisato Shunchosai Takehara 1797

Edición en Inglés | de Cristina Berna y Eric Thomsen

Sin reseñas

Tapa blanda

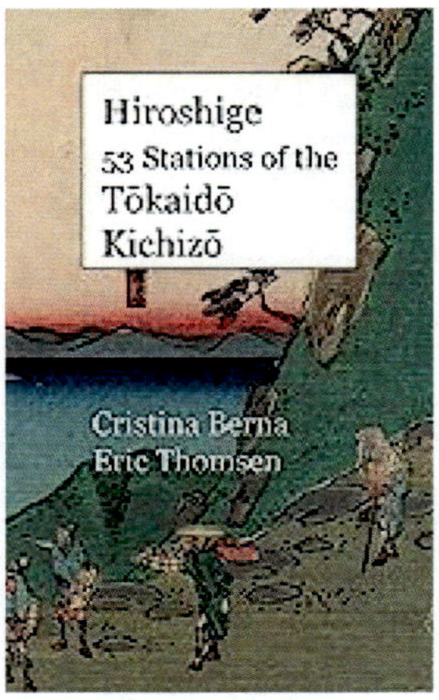

Hiroshige 53 Stations of the Tōkaidō Kichizō: Premium

Edición en Inglés | de Cristina Berna y Eric Thomsen

2,0*2,0 de 5 estrellas* (5)

Tapa dura

Hiroshige 36 Views of Mt Fuji 1852: Premium

Edición en Inglés | de Cristina Berna y Eric Thomsen

2,7*2,7 de 5 estrellas* (4)

Tapa dura

El museo de esfuerzos inútiles

Edición en Inglés | de Cristina Peri Rossi

5,0*5,0 de 5 estrellas* (2)

Tapa blanda

¿Necesitas ayuda?

Visita la sección de ayuda o ponte en contacto con nosotros

(only books included...)

Search link (7 Apr 2023) is

https://www.amazon.es/s?k=cristina+berna&me=A1894GFVA6IFD7&__mk_es_ES=%C3%85M%C3%85%C5%BD%C3%95%C3%91&ref=nb_sb_noss

Only the first one – the Joaquin Sorolla Nudes – is a “legal” title re-issued through our agent – the others are the versions “cancelled” by Ingram without proper cause abt two years ago, but being sold by Amazon and its “trusted sellers” apparently as counterfeit versions?

Neither Amazon nor any of the “trusted sellers” give sales information or pay author´s fee – not upon request and not just by themselves.

All our books sold by DMI Media Europe are “second hand, as good as new”.

This means either they have a huge, huge, huge warehouse full of old books.....or they are specialized in second hand versions of our books....,

It may also be a technical labelling thing like Trump and "falsification of business records"....???

Maybe there is another hand between the press and the guy from DMI??...handing the book over to him from the press???

It would certainly be a great idea to go and see this huge, huge warehouse where all these old books are. A book mortuary!

You think it is only our books?

Look here – the first of the 200,000 books offered by DMI Media Europe...

UPDATED +
EXPANDED
INTERNATIONAL
BESTSELLER
THE
FIRST
90
DAYS
Proven Strategies for Getting Up
to Speed Faster and Smarter
MICHAEL D. WATKINS
HARVARD BUSINESS REVIEW PRESS

Sigue al autor

Michael Watkins

Seguir

The First 90 Days. Updated And Expanded: Proven Straegies for Getting up to Speed

faster and smarter Tapa dura – 14 mayo 2013

Edición en Inglés de Michael Watkins (Autor, Colaborador)

*4,5 de 5 estrellas_* 9.628 valoraciones

Ver todos los formatos y ediciones

- Versión Kindle
  15,99 €Leer con nuestra **App gratuita**

- **Tapa dura**
  35,89 €
  Otros de 2ª mano a partir de 35,89 €

Detalles del producto

- **Editorial** : N/E; Updated and expanded edition (14 mayo 2013)
- **Idioma** : Inglés
- **Tapa dura** : 1 páginas
- **ISBN-10** : 1422188612
- **ISBN-13** : 978-1422188613
- **Peso del producto** : 349 g
- **Dimensiones** : 14.61 x 3.18 x 21.59 cm

- **Clasificación en los más vendidos de Amazon:** nº142 en Empresa, estrategia y gestión (Libros)
    - nº274 en Libros en inglés
    - nº294 en Libros en idiomas extranjeros
- **Opiniones de los clientes:**
  *4,5 de 5 estrellas_* 9.628 valoraciones

The offer in a drop-down is

De 2ª mano - Como nuevo

35,89 €35,89€

Entrega por 5,75 € entre el **10 - 31 de mayo**. Ver detalles

Submit Añadir a la cesta

Estado

Producto enviado desde los Estados Unidos. Tenemos un servicio al cliente disponible. No vacilen en man... Más

Envía por

DMI Media Europe

Vendedor

DMI Media Europe

(50 calificaciones)
69 % positivas en los últimos 12 meses

The link is (7 Apr 2023)

https://www.amazon.es/First-90-Days-Updated-Expanded/dp/1422188612/ref=sr_1_1?m=A1894GFVA6IFD7&marketplaceID=A1RKKUPIHCS9HS&qid=1680882806&s=merchant-items&sr=1-1

Oh, and there are several others offering the book “second hand, as good as new”. Incl Amazon itself.

Let us go to the 14th book we have uploaded via our agent

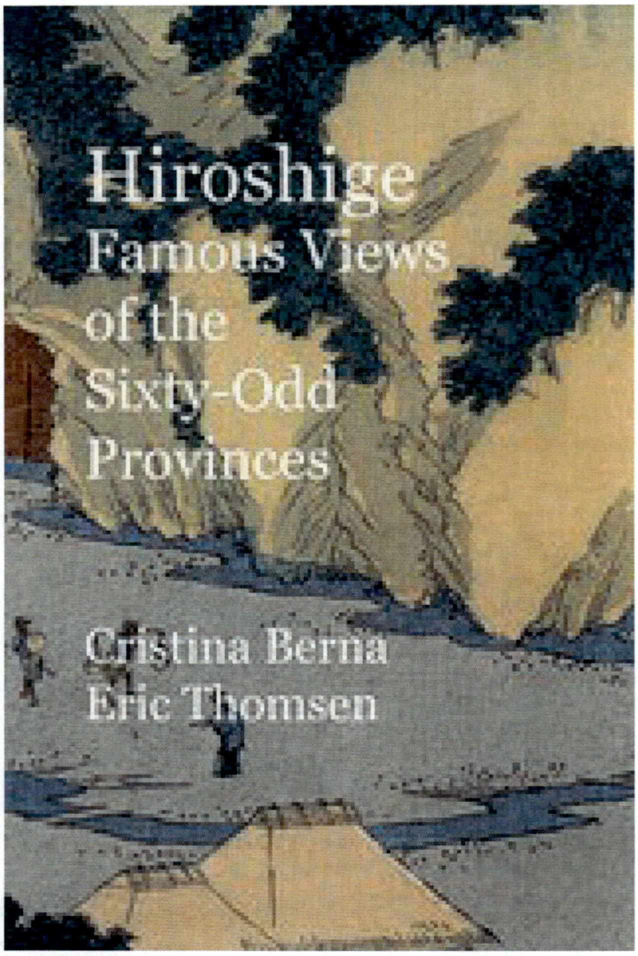

[***Hiroshige FamousViews of the Sixty-Odd Province***]()

Cristina Berna Precio 99.95€ ISBN 978-1-956773-99-6

This book was uploaded 28 Dec 2022, so this is more than three months ago, like with the previous title, meaning this is not something Amazon has not been able to adjust in a timely fashion.

The book also has a link in the our agent system to an Amazon.es page

Plataforma	Enlace
ama	https://www.amazon.es/s/ref=nb_sb_noss?__mk_es_ES=%C3%85M%C3%85%C5%BD%C3%95%C3%91&url=search-alias%3Daps&field-keywords=9781956773996

If you click this link you get the following information:

1 resultado para **"9781956773996"**

Ordenar por:

Lanzamientos recientes

Ordenar por:Destacados

Resultados

Más información sobre estos resultados.

Hiroshige Famous Views of the Sixty-Odd Provinces

Edición en Inglés
de Cristina Berna

Nuevo en Amazon

Tapa blanda

99,95€ 99,95€

Entrega por 5,68 € el **mi., 5 de abr.**

Otro formato: Tapa dura

Again, you note there is a link to "tapa dura", to other versions of our book.

Amazon is filtering in these link onto the book pages for the new legal versions we re-issue via our agent.

If you click on the link Tapa dura you get the following result

The link 7 Apr 2023 is

https://www.amazon.es/Hiroshige-Famous-Views-Sixty-Odd-Provinces/dp/1647863252/ref=sr_1_1?__mk_es_ES=%C3%85M%C3%85%C5%BD%C3%95%C3%91&keywords=9781956773996&qid=1680885694&sr=8-1

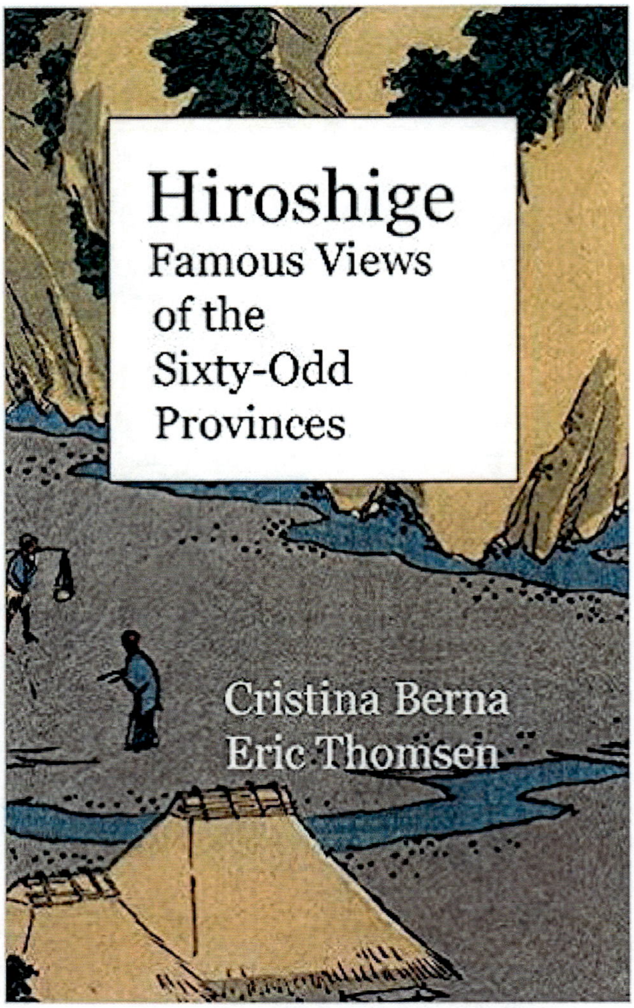
Hiroshige
Famous Views
of the
Sixty-Odd
Provinces
Cristina Berna
Eric Thomsen

Hiroshige Famous Views of the Sixty-Odd Provinces Tapa dura – 16 enero 2020

Edición en Inglés de Cristina Berna (Autor)

Sin reseñas

Ver todos los formatos y ediciones

- **Tapa dura**
  —
- Tapa blanda
  78,34 €
  Otros nuevo a partir de 78,34 €

Detalles del producto

- **Idioma** : Inglés
- **ISBN-10** : 1647863252
- **ISBN-13** : 978-1647863258
- **Peso del producto** : 360 g
- **Dimensiones** : 15.24 x 1.27 x 22.86 cm

But the hardcover is not available.

Instead there is a link to paperback

Otros nuevo a partir de 78,34 €

Click on that and you get the following offers as a drop-down without link

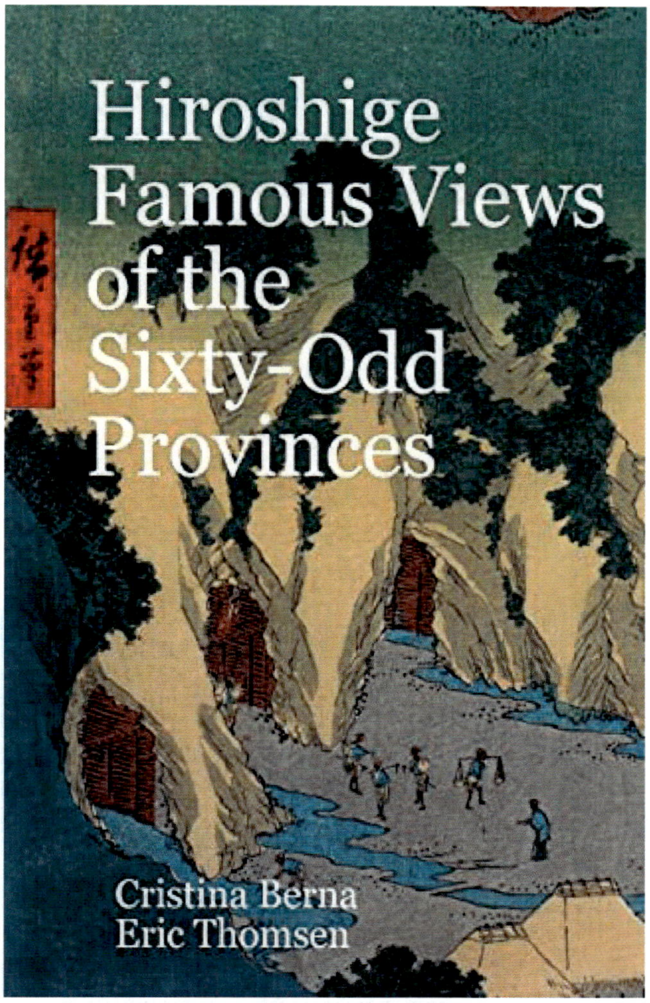

Hiroshige Famous Views of the Sixty-Odd Provinces
Tapa blanda

Nuevo
78,34€ 78,34€

5,64 € entrega

Submit Añadir a la cesta

Envía por

Amazon

Vendedor

Amazon

Ver menos

Nuevo

113,00€ 113,00€

Entrega por 5,64 € entre el **18 - 26 de abril**. Ver detalles

Submit Añadir a la cesta

Envía por

ALLBOOKS_

Vendedor

ALLBOOKS_

Nuevo vendedor

But what are they offering?

Click on the link

Ver todos los formatos y ediciones

And you get the answer:

Tapa dura
(1)
Tapa blanda
(2)

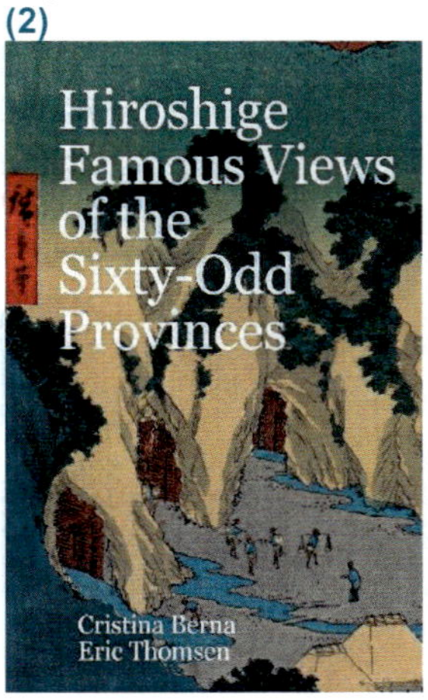

Hiroshige Famous Views of the Sixty-Odd Provinces

78,34€ €78,34

Nuevo desde 78,34 €

Calificación	(0)
ISBN-13	978-1956773699
Editor	Missys Clan
Fecha de publicación	14 septiembre 2022

Hiroshige Famous Views of the Sixty-Odd Provinces

99,95€ €99,95

Nuevo desde 99,95 €

Calificación	(0)
ISBN-13	978-1956773996
Fecha de publicación	28 diciembre 2022

The cheap offer gives the new ISBN number for the book uploaded with our agent, but it gives a wrong re-issue date.

It is necessary to investigate, was this just a little mistake, or is the book actually a counterfeit?

You see, the list price is €99.95 – so how can Amazon offer this book at a lower price?

Nuevo

78,34€ 78,34€

Is it really our new book or is it a copy of it?

In the old Philip Kotler book on Marketing, an executive of Montgomery Ward was quoted for saying:

"We lose a bit on every sale, but BOY do we have a volume!!"

Let us look now at the 15th book uploaded to our agent:

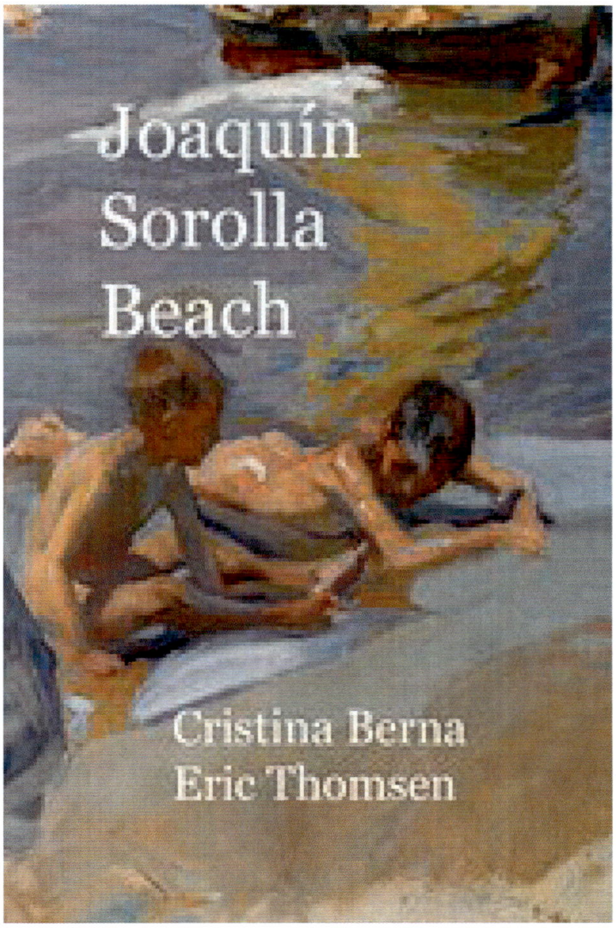

Joaquín Sorolla Beach

Cristina Berna Precio 49.95€ ISBN 978-1-960269-00-3

It was uploaded 28 Dec 2022. As you saw under the Spanish edition, it was our first book about the wonderful paintings by Joaquin Sorolla.

The book has a link to a book page in Amazon according to our agent:

Enlaces

Plataforma	Enlace
am	https://www.amazon.es/s/ref=nb_sb_noss?__mk_es_ES=%C3%85M%C3%85%C5%BD%C3%95%C3%91&url=search-alias%3Daps&field-keywords=9781960269003

If you click this link, you get the following information

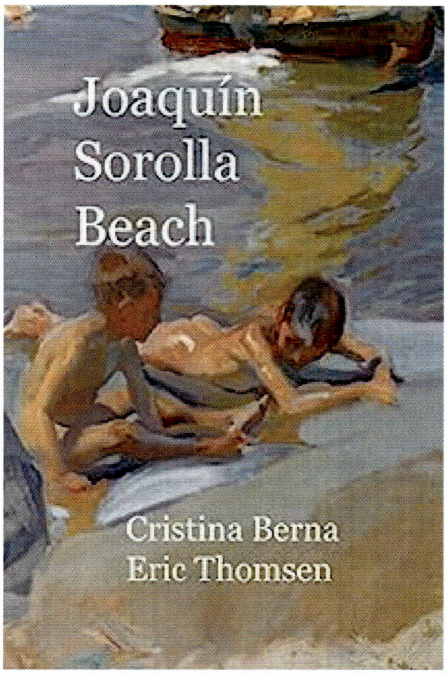

Joaquín Sorolla Beach

Edición en Inglés

de Cristina Berna

1,0*1,0 de 5 estrellas* (2)

[Tapa blanda]

49,95€ 49,95€

Entrega por 5,66 € el **ju., 13 de abr.**

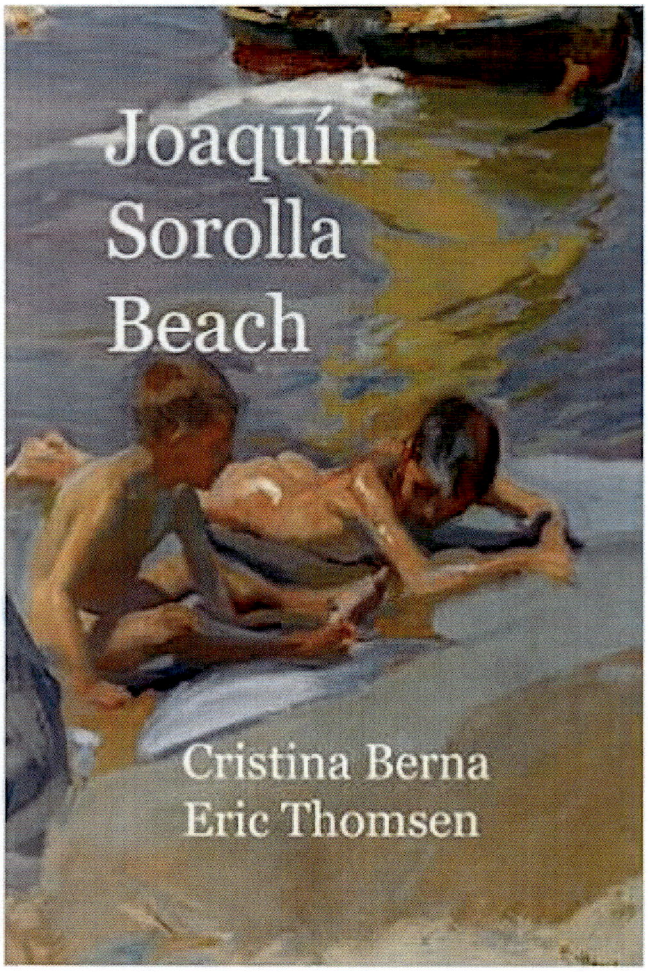
Joaquín
Sorolla
Beach
Cristina Berna
Eric Thomsen

Joaquín Sorolla Beach Tapa blanda – 28 diciembre 2022

Edición en Inglés de Cristina Berna (Autor)

1,0 de 5 estrellas 2 valoraciones

Ver todos los formatos y ediciones

- **Tapa blanda**
  49,95 €
  Otros nuevo a partir de 49,95 €

Detalles del producto

- **Editorial** : VESTERNAES (28 diciembre 2022)
- **Idioma** : Inglés
- **Tapa blanda** : 160 páginas
- **ISBN-10** : 1960269003
- **ISBN-13** : 978-1960269003
- **Peso del producto** : 259 g
- **Dimensiones** : 14 x 0.94 x 21 cm
- **Opiniones de los clientes:**
  1,0 de 5 estrellas 2 valoraciones

The link is

https://www.amazon.es/Joaqu%C3%ADn-Sorolla-Beach-Cristina-Berna/dp/1960269003/ref=sr_1_1?__mk_es_ES=%C3%85M%C3%85%C5%BD%C3%95%C3%91&keywords=9781960269003&qid=1680887405&sr=8-1

There is no information to or linking to the Spanish version

The link is Ver todos los formatos y ediciones

And you get this result

Tapa blanda
(1)

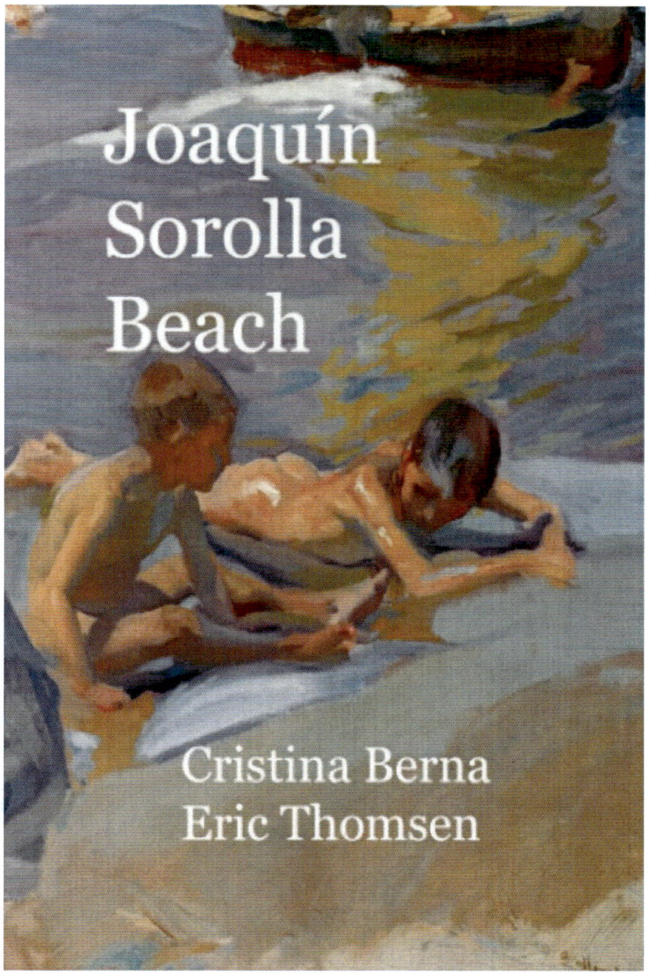

Joaquín Sorolla Beach

49,95€ €49,95

Nuevo desde 49,95 €

Calificación	(0)
ISBN-13	978-1960269003

The offering is

Otros nuevo a partir de 49,95 €

Nuevo

49,95€ 49,95€

by Amazon.

There are two reviews – we already saw them earlier when we looked at the Spanish version in our agent – they have been carried over from the 2019 version that Ingram “cancelled”.

If you do a general search on Amazon, title+author specific you get this result

5 resultados para **"cristina berna joaquin sorolla beach"**

Ordenar por:

Precio: De mayor a menor

Ordenar por: Destacados

Resultados

Más información sobre estos resultados.

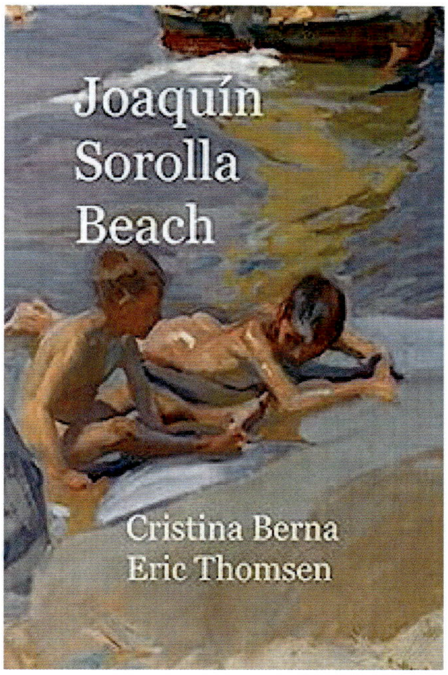

Joaquín Sorolla Beach
Edición en Inglés
de Cristina Berna

1,0*1,0 de 5 estrellas* (2)

Tapa blanda

49,95€ 49,95€

Entrega por 5,66 € el **ju., 13 de abr.**

Joaquín Sorolla Beach More

Edición en Inglés

de Cristina Berna

2,0*2,0 de 5 estrellas* (1)

Tapa blanda

75,95€ 75,95€

PVPR: 79,95 €79,95€

Entrega por 5,67 € el **mi., 12 de abr.**

Joaquín Sorolla Beach More: Premium

Edición en Inglés

de Cristina Berna y Eric Thomsen

1,0*1,0 de 5 estrellas* (1)

Tapa dura

No disponible.

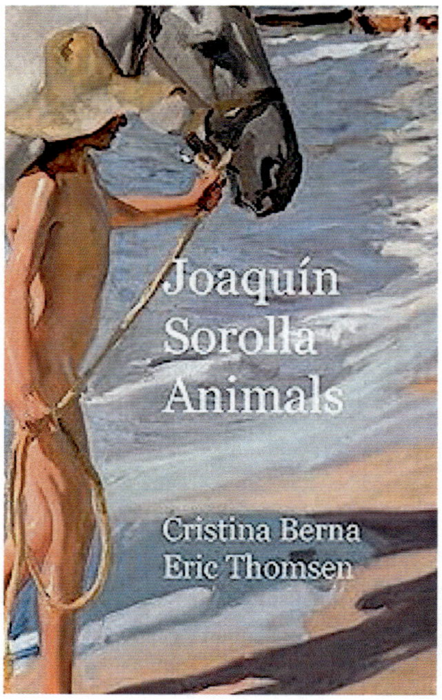

Joaquin Sorolla Animals

Edición en Inglés

de Cristina Berna

1,0*1,0 de 5 estrellas* (1)

Tapa dura

34,99€ 34,99€

PVPR: 93,71 €93,71€

Entrega por 6,99 € entre el **25 de abr. - 17 de my.**

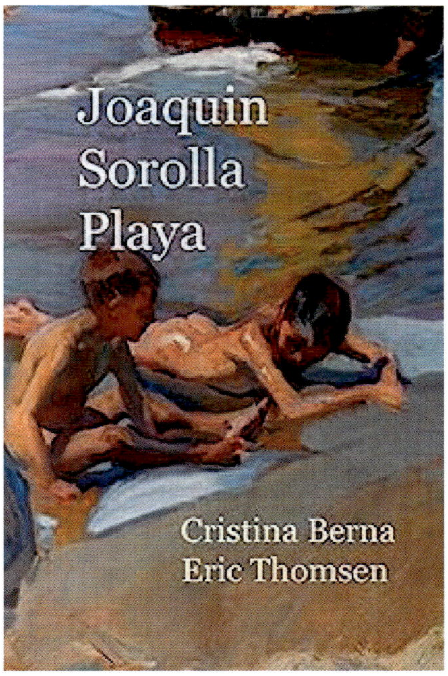

Joaquin Sorolla Playa

de Cristina Berna y Eric Thomsen

2,0*2,0 de 5 estrellas* (1)

Tapa blanda

79,95€ 79,95€

Entrega por 5,66 € el **ju., 13 de abr.**

Más opciones de compra

74,35 € (2 o fertas usadas y nuevas)

The link to this search 7 Apr 2023 is

https://www.amazon.es/s?k=cristina+berna+joaquin+sorolla+beach&__mk_es_ES=%C3%85M%C3%85%C5%BD%C3%95%C3%91&crid=1R4Y48XS11A6R&sprefix=cristina+berna+joaquin+sorolla+beach%2Caps%2C136&ref=nb_sb_noss

Let us go to the last book, the 16th of the first 16 uploaded to our agent

Joauín Sorolla Family

Cristina Berna Precio 99.95€ ISBN 978-1-960269-13-3

This book was uploaded 28 Dec 2022.

It has a link to a book page in amazon.es

Enlaces

Plataforma	Enlace
am	https://www.amazon.es/s/ref=nb_sb_noss?__mk_es_ES=%C3%85M%C3%85%C5%BD%C3%95%C3%91&url=search-alias%3Daps&field-keywords=9781960269010

If you click this link you get the following information

Más información sobre estos resultados.

Joaquín Sorolla Family

Edición en Inglés

de Cristina Berna

3,0*3,0 de 5 estrellas* (1)

Tapa blanda

75,95€ 75,95€

PVPR: 79,95 €79,95€

Entrega por 5,73 € el **mi., 12 de abr.**

If you click the link **Tapa blanda** you get this page

https://www.amazon.es/Joaqu%C3%ADn-Sorolla-Family-Cristina-Berna/dp/1960269011/ref=sr_1_1?__mk_es_ES=%C3%85M%C3%85%C5%BD%C3%95%C3%91&keywords=9781960269010&qid=1680889001&sr=8-1#customerReviews

There is a review and it is very nice...thank you very much!

UK Customer

3,0 de 5 estrellas **Wonderful painter, but poor quality printing**

Revisado en Reino Unido el 3 de abril de 2021

Compra verificada

A master painter. A very engaging book. I loved the book and read it cover to cover in a few hours. Not translated by a native speaker of English, yet this might add to its charm. The printing is poor quality. It also has many many printing mistakes, it should have been proof read by a professional proof-reader before it went to print.

A una persona le ha parecido esto útil

Denunciar

Traducir reseña a Español

Here again you see the authors are blamed for the poor quality printing.

The reviewer could not know that we deliberately kept many Spanish names of the paintings so as to make it easier to find them in Spain. The book will come in a Spanish version as well – soon.

The book is offered new by Amazon slightly below list price, but when you add shipping charge, it is abt the same.

If you do a general search on amazon author-title specific, you get this result

4 resultados para **"cristina berna joaquin sorolla family"**

Ordenar por:

Lanzamientos recientes

Ordenar por:Destacados

Resultados

Más información sobre estos resultados.

Joaquín Sorolla Family

Edición en Inglés

de Cristina Berna

3,0*3,0 de 5 estrellas* (1)

Tapa blanda

75,95€ 75,95€

PVPR: 79,95 €79,95€

Entrega por 5,73 € el **mi., 12 de abr.**

Joaquin Sorolla Family

Edición en Inglés

de Cristina Berna

4,0*4,0 de 5 estrellas* (1)

Tapa dura

No disponible.

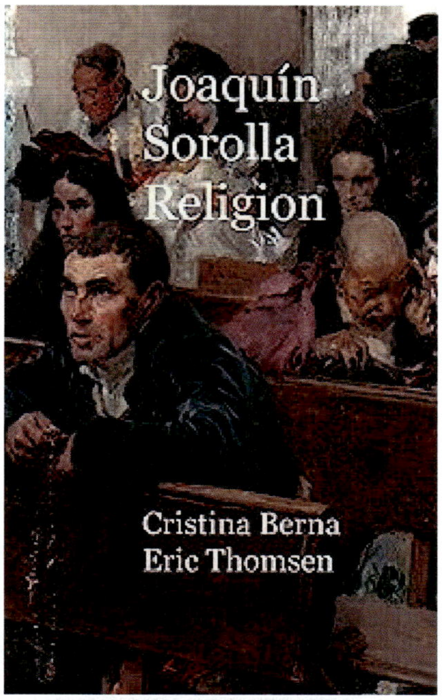

Joaquín Sorolla Religion: Premium
Edición en Inglés
de Cristina Berna y Eric Thomsen

Sin reseñas

Tapa dura

No disponible.

Lakabara por Citon Joaquin Sorolla 《Coser la Vela》 Lienzo Pinturas artísticas Obra de Arte Impresión Giclee Telón de Fondo Decoración de Pared Decoración del hogar Póster 30x40cm Sin Marco
Poliéster

Sin reseñas

23,00€ 23,00€

Entrega por 6,10 € entre el **20 de abr. - 12 de my.**

Opciones:

5 tamaños5 tamaños

Utilice menos palabras clave o pruebe con estas

cristina berna joaquin sorollaVer los 18 resultados

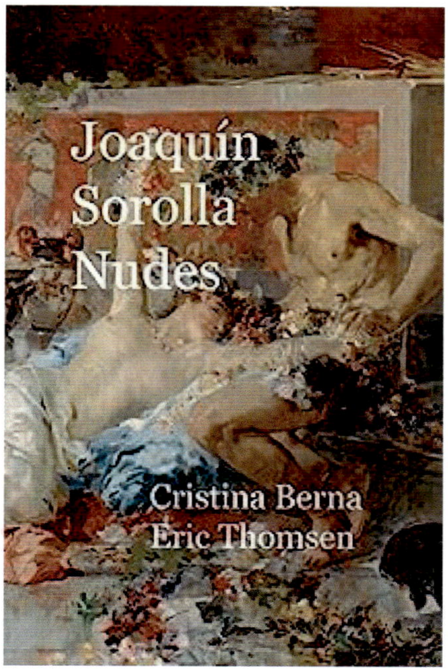

Joaquín Sorolla Nudes

Edición en Inglés

de Cristina Berna

1,4*1,4 de 5 estrellas* (3)

Tapa blanda

79,95€ 79,95€

Entrega por 5,68 € el **mi., 12 de abr.**

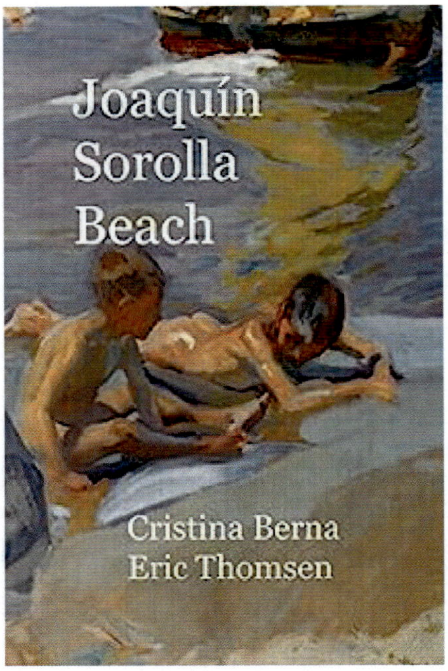

Joaquín Sorolla Beach
Edición en Inglés
de Cristina Berna

1,0*1,0 de 5 estrellas* (2)

Tapa blanda

49,95€ 49,95€

Entrega por 5,66 € el **ju., 13 de abr.**

The link to the search 7 Apr 2023 is

https://www.amazon.es/s?k=cristina+berna+joaquin+sorolla+family&__mk_es_ES=%C3%85M%C3%85%C5%BD%C3%95%C3%91&crid=4TEGK6JY5QEU&sprefix=cristina+berna+joaquin+sorolla+family%2Caps%2C112&ref=nb_sb_noss

If you go to the hardcover, the one "cancelled" by Ingram for no proper reason abt two years ago – there is also a valuation – four stars out of five, which is very nice for us.

As you see, Amazon throws in an advertisement for a painting, a copy of one of Sorolla´s paintings – the sailmakers – repairing the sail. We don´t have anything to do with that.

Amazon also shows the "Joaquin Sorolla Religion", another of our books and one which is very relevant for Spanish family values.

Now we have analysed the 16 books in Amazon, from a certain angle, and shown other aspects.

Amazon Prime delivery trucks, Gainesville, Florida, image: TaurusEmerald

“Paketband Online Handel Amazon Box”, image: Benzoyl

Resume

Based on the journey on Amazon´s site for 16 of our books we can distill some points

- Amazon and its "trusted sellers" dump prices apparently even to below printing costs to get customers to switch from us

- Amazon is sometimes not giving a book page with a link although this is promised by the agent

- Amazon is sometimes claiming a title is "unavailable" instead of providing a link to the lawful title

- Amazon is sometimes providing links to paperback versions they offer for sale but that are "cancelled" by Ingram abt two years ago instead of providing a link to the lawful version

- Amazon is sometimes dumping the price of the lawful copy by offering a "cancelled" version at a – sometimes very considerable – lower price

- Amazon is not providing sales statistics or statistics on accrued author´s fees

- nor is Amazon paying any such fees to the authors for the two years since Ingram “cancelled” all authors 291 titles

- Amazon and its “trusted sellers” are not providing copies of invoices showing lawful purchase of the “cancelled” titles which were “cancelled” by Ingram abt two years ago

- neither on “new” or “second hand, as new” copies offered for sale

- one “trusted seller” is offering 200,000 “second hand, as new” books for sale by multiple authors in the Amazon operated “storefront”

- Amazon is operating a large, international network of “trusted sellers” who have “storefronts” inside the Amazon website

- these “trusted sellers” are difficult to contact and it would be time consuming and cost prohibitive to do so for most authors

- Amazon and its network of “trusted sellers” are offering a large number of our 291 “cancelled” work, cancelled by Ingram abt two years ago

- These works are sparsed out among the “trusted sellers” so no one has more than a few on offer, but in aggregate Amazon and this network appears to be “fishing” with the total list of 291 “cancelled” works

- In this way it appears to be a strategy not to attract too much attention to one single “trusted seller” that he offers many of our “cancelled” works for sale

- Amazon is letting customers write reviews that blame us for poor print quality

- Amazon is not letting us rebut on their website

- Amazon is allegedly printing our books themselves from pdf files downloaded from an agent

- Amazon and its network of “trusted sellers” appear to be engaged in willful and intentional disregard of the copyright statement contained in each every single of the works they sell, even those that are “cancelled” by Ingram abt two years ago

- Amazon and its “trusted sellers” appear to hold a considerable stock of our works that were “cancelled” by Ingram abt two years ago, in spite of no bulk sales having been reported by Ingram prior to “cancellation” and no sales after that

- Amazon and its network of “trusted sellers” are offering this large number of “cancelled” works for sale at prices lower than what they originally would have been able to acquire them for and in some cases at or below printing costs

- The business model of Amazon and its network of “trusted sellers” appears to be:

buy at full price, store large numbers of copies for extended periods and sell them at huge discounts

- indicating this could be a money laundering scheme

- Amazon is sometimes not giving search results directly or in the “storefronts” of their “trusted sellers”

- but the “hits” pop up in drop-downs with no links, deep inside these un-linked drop-downs, on specific nook version pages

- and sometimes with “new to Amazon” “trusted sellers”

- long delivery times – up to a month – for many works “cancelled” by Ingram abt two years ago point to the books having to be printed first, not being in physical stock, and maybe hand-made

- Some of our books appear to simply be “banned” (blocked”, not showing) on Amazon to suppress sales and income

- Links to alleged counterfeit version of our books are “filtered” onto the book pages of our lawfully offered books e.g. with links to “hardcover” which are “cancelled” by Ingram abt two years ago but still offered for sale by Amazon and its network of “trusted sellers”

- thus drawing traffic away from the legal versions and

- drawing sales over to allegedly counterfeit works which are even sold at considerably lower prices

- All these tactics appear to be willful and deliberate to depress sales and income opportunities for the authors

- Amazon shows that when it suits Amazon it is perfectly capable of providing correct information on our books

- Lawfully available books are sometimes listed as “unavailable” to depress sales causing loss of income to authors and their agent

- Amazon appears to deliver poor printing quality at full price and with no discount and to let authors bear the criticism for the poor printing

- Amazon sometimes shunt author specific searches to other (better selling? or inducement paying?) authors causing loss of sales and income opportunities

- Amazon is expanding its network of "trusted sellers"

Street vendors, Puerta del Sol, Madrid. Image: Artibus3

Seattle Streetcar vehicle 407, in an orange Amazon Prime advertisement wrap, seen leaving the southern terminus of the South Lake Union Streetcar on a snowy day. 2019. Image: SounderBruce

Image: Parnell27

Discussion

Now we can give some further comments.

The question is:

How many counterfeit books do Amazon and its "trusted sellers" sell?

How many have they sold since Ingram "cancelled" our books for no good reason abt two years ago?

Is it

200 books

2.000 books

20.000 books

200.000 books

????

Amazon has this information available, listed by ISBN number – they could just furnish it if they wanted.

The next question is –

How many other authors get the same treatment?

Is it

200 authors

2.000 authors

20.000 authors

200.000 authors`

????

Again, Amazon has this information – it has probably also been given to the Board of Directors and to the legal department.

So, how many books have been sold as counterfeit and for how long?

Let us just say Amazon has sold between 200 and 2.000 of our books since Ingram "cancelled" our book list.

Let us say Amazon has kept $20 per book on average – some they give away we have seen.

Let us say an average of 1.100 books then at $20 a piece, this is $22.000.00

Let us say there are 20.000 authors in the same situation

or

$440.000.000 over these two years.

That would be enough to sink Amazon, right?

So, should you buy Amazon stock?

Then there are some more moral and legal issues – both the buying and the systematic selling of counterfeit goods is criminalized.

Could you as a customer get into trouble if an investigation was launched?

Amazon has the sales records, your name, your credit card information, everything.

The authorities could just print a letter with a fine, based on Amazon´s customer information.

It could save a country from bankruptcy....

Book flea market on Cuesta de Moyano, Madrid, Spain. Image: Ecemaml

Case law

Legal framework in the European for Member States´ legislation, overview cited in:

Case C-597/19 10 Dec 2020

Mircom International Content Management & Consulting (M.I.C.M.) Limited v Telenet BVBA,

Legal framework

7. The request for a preliminary ruling in the present case contains no description of the national legal framework. I shall confine myself, therefore, in this part of the Opinion, to setting out the EU legal framework. It will be for the national court to adapt the interpretation of that law given by the Court to its own national legal framework.

Intellectual property law

8. Under Article 3(1) and (2)(c) of Directive 2001/29/EC of the European Parliament and of the Council of 22 May 2001 on the harmonisation of certain aspects of copyright and related rights in the information society: (5)

> '1. Member States shall provide for the exclusive right to authorise or prohibit the making available to the public, by wire or wireless means, in such a way that members of the public may access them from a place and at a time individually chosen by them.

2. Member States shall provide for the exclusive right to authorise or prohibit the making available to the public, by wire or wireless means, in such a way that members of the public may access them from a place and at a time individually chosen by them:

...

(c) for the producers of the first fixations of films, of the original and copies of their films;

...'

9. In accordance with Article 8 of that directive:

'1. Member States shall provide appropriate sanctions and remedies in respect of infringements of the rights and obligations set out in this Directive and shall take all the measures necessary to ensure that those sanctions and remedies are applied. The sanctions thus provided for shall be effective, proportionate and dissuasive.

2. Each Member State shall take the measures necessary to ensure that rightholders whose interests are affected by an infringing activity carried out on its territory can bring an action for damages and/or apply for an injunction and, where appropriate, for the seizure of infringing material as well as of devices, products or components referred to in Article 6(2).

3. Member States shall ensure that rightholders are in a position to apply for an injunction against intermediaries whose services are used by a third party to infringe a copyright or related right.'

10. Article 2 of Directive 2004/48/EC of the European Parliament and of the Council of 29 April 2004 on the enforcement of intellectual property rights (6) provides:

> '1. Without prejudice to the means which are or may be provided for in [EU] or national legislation, in so far as those means may be more favourable for rightholders, the measures, procedures and remedies provided for by this Directive shall apply, in accordance with Article 3, to any infringement of intellectual property rights as provided for by [EU] law and/or by the national law of the Member State concerned.
>
> 2. This Directive shall be without prejudice to the specific provisions on the enforcement of rights and on exceptions contained in [EU] legislation concerning copyright and rights related to copyright, notably those found ... in Directive [2001/29] and, in particular, ... Article 8 thereof.
>
> 3. This Directive shall not affect:
>
> (a) ... Directive 95/46/EC [(7)] ...
>
> ...'

11. Chapter II of that directive governs the 'measures, procedures and remedies' necessary to ensure the enforcement of intellectual property rights. Under Article 3 of that directive:

> '1. Member States shall provide for the measures, procedures and remedies necessary to ensure the enforcement of the intellectual property rights covered by this Directive. Those measures, procedures and remedies shall be fair and equitable

and shall not be unnecessarily complicated or costly, or entail unreasonable time limits or unwarranted delays.

2. Those measures, procedures and remedies shall also be effective, proportionate and dissuasive and shall be applied in such a manner as to avoid the creation of barriers to legitimate trade and to provide for safeguards against their abuse.'

12. Article 4 of that directive provides:

'Member States shall recognise as persons entitled to seek application of the measures, procedures and remedies referred to in this Chapter:

(a) the holders of intellectual property rights, in accordance with the provisions of the applicable law,

(b) all other persons authorised to use those rights, in particular licensees, in so far as permitted by and in accordance with the provisions of the applicable law,

(c) intellectual property collective rights management bodies which are regularly recognised as having a right to represent holders of intellectual property rights, in so far as permitted by and in accordance with the provisions of the applicable law,

(d) professional defence bodies which are regularly recognised as having a right to represent holders of intellectual property rights, in so far as permitted by and in accordance with the provisions of the applicable law.'

13. Under Article 8 of Directive 2004/48:

> '1. Member States shall ensure that, in the context of proceedings concerning an infringement of an intellectual property right and in response to a justified and proportionate request of the claimant, the competent judicial authorities may order that information on the origin and distribution networks of the goods or services which infringe an intellectual property right be provided by the infringer and/or any other person who:
>
> ...
>
> (c) was found to be providing on a commercial scale services used in infringing activities; or
>
> ...
>
> 2. The information referred to in paragraph 1 shall, as appropriate, comprise:
>
> (a) the names and addresses of the producers, manufacturers, distributors, suppliers and other previous holders of the goods or services, as well as the intended wholesalers and retailers;
>
> ...
>
> 3. Paragraphs 1 and 2 shall apply without prejudice to other statutory provisions which:
>
> ...
>
> (e) govern the protection of confidentiality of information sources or the processing of personal data.'

14. Finally, under Article 13(1) and (2) of that directive:

> '1. Member States shall ensure that the competent judicial authorities, on application of the injured party, order the infringer who knowingly, or with reasonable grounds to know, engaged in an infringing activity, to pay the rightholder damages appropriate to the actual prejudice suffered by him/her as a result of the infringement.
>
> ...
>
> 2. Where the infringer did not knowingly, or with reasonable grounds to know, engage in infringing activity, Member States may lay down that the judicial authorities may order the recovery of profits or the payment of damages, which may be pre-established.'

Electronic communications law

15. Under Article 2(a) and (c) of Directive 2002/21/EC of the European Parliament and of the Council of 7 March 2002 on a common regulatory framework for electronic communications networks and services (Framework Directive), (8) as amended by Directive 2009/140/EC of the European Parliament and of the Council of 25 November 2009 (9) ('Directive 2002/21'):

> 'For the purposes of this Directive:
>
> (a) "electronic communications network" means transmission systems and, where applicable, switching or routing equipment and other resources, including network elements which are not active, which permit the conveyance of signals by wire, radio, optical or other electromagnetic means, including satellite

networks, fixed (circuit- and packet-switched, including Internet) and mobile terrestrial networks, electricity cable systems, to the extent that they are used for the purpose of transmitting signals, networks used for radio and television broadcasting, and cable television networks, irrespective of the type of information conveyed;

...

(c) "electronic communications service" means a service normally provided for remuneration which consists wholly or mainly in the conveyance of signals on electronic communications networks, including telecommunications services and transmission services in networks used for broadcasting, but exclude services providing, or exercising editorial control over, content transmitted using electronic communications networks and services; it does not include information society services, as defined in Article 1 of Directive 98/34/EC, [(10)] which do not consist wholly or mainly in the conveyance of signals on electronic communications networks;'

16. Article 1(1) and (2) of Directive 2002/58/EC of the European Parliament and of the Council of 12 July 2002 concerning the processing of personal data and the protection of privacy in the electronic communications sector (Directive on privacy and electronic communications), (11) as amended by Directive 2009/136/EC of the European Parliament and of the Council of 25 November 2009 (12) ('Directive 2002/58'), provides:

'1. This Directive provides for the harmonisation of the national provisions required to ensure an equivalent level of protection of fundamental rights and freedoms, and in particular the right to privacy and confidentiality, with respect to the processing of personal data in the electronic communication sector and to ensure the free movement of such data and of electronic communication equipment and services in the [Union].

2. The provisions of this Directive particularise and complement Directive [95/46] for the purposes mentioned in paragraph 1. ...'

17. Under Article 2 of Directive 2002/58:

'Save as otherwise provided, the definitions in Directive [95/46] and in Directive [2002/21] shall apply.

The following definitions shall also apply:

(a) "user" means any natural person using a publicly available electronic communications service, for private or business purposes, without necessarily having subscribed to this service;

(b) "traffic data" means any data processed for the purpose of the conveyance of a communication on an electronic communications network or for the billing thereof;

...

(d) "communication" means any information exchanged or conveyed between a finite

> number of parties by means of a publicly available electronic communications service. ...'

18. In accordance with Article 5(1) of that directive:

> 'Member States shall ensure the confidentiality of communications and the related traffic data by means of a public communications network and publicly available electronic communications services, through national legislation. In particular, they shall prohibit listening, tapping, storage or other kinds of interception or surveillance of communications and the related traffic data by persons other than users, without the consent of the users concerned, except when legally authorised to do so in accordance with Article 15(1). This paragraph shall not prevent technical storage which is necessary for the conveyance of a communication without prejudice to the principle of confidentiality.'

19. Article 6(1) of that directive provides:

> 'Traffic data relating to subscribers and users processed and stored by the provider of a public communications network or publicly available electronic communications service must be erased or made anonymous when it is no longer needed for the purpose of the transmission of a communication without prejudice to paragraphs 2, 3 and 5 of this Article and Article 15(1).'

20. Finally, under Article 15(1) of that directive:

> 'Member States may adopt legislative measures to restrict the scope of the rights and obligations provided for in Article 5, Article 6 ... of this Directive

when such restriction constitutes a necessary, appropriate and proportionate measure within a democratic society to safeguard national security (i.e. State security), defence, public security, and the prevention, investigation, detection and prosecution of criminal offences or of unauthorised use of the electronic communication system, as referred to in Article 13(1) of Directive [95/46]. To this end, Member States may, inter alia, adopt legislative measures providing for the retention of data for a limited period justified on the grounds laid down in this paragraph. All the measures referred to in this paragraph shall be in accordance with the general principles of [Union] law, including those referred to in Article 6(1) and (2) of the Treaty on European Union.'

General provisions on the protection of personal data

21. Article 4(1), (2), (7) and (9) of Regulation (EU) 2016/679 of the European Parliament and of the Council of 27 April 2016 on the protection of natural persons with regard to the processing of personal data and on the free movement of such data, and repealing Directive 95/46/EC (General Data Protection Regulation), (13) provides:

'For the purposes of this Regulation:

(1) "personal data" means any information relating to an identified or identifiable natural person ("data subject"); an identifiable natural person is one who can be identified, directly or indirectly, in particular by reference to an identifier such as a name, an identification number, location data, an online identifier or to one or more factors specific to the physical, physiological, genetic, mental, economic,

cultural or social identity of that natural person;

(2) "processing" means any operation or set of operations which is performed on personal data or on sets of personal data, whether or not by automated means, such as collection, recording, organisation, structuring, storage, adaptation or alteration, retrieval, consultation, use, disclosure by transmission, dissemination or otherwise making available, alignment or combination, restriction, erasure or destruction;

...

(7) "controller" means the natural or legal person, public authority, agency or other body which, alone or jointly with others, determines the purposes and means of the processing of personal data; where the purposes and means of such processing are determined by Union or Member State law, the controller or the specific criteria for its nomination may be provided for by Union or Member State law;

...

(9) "recipient" means a natural or legal person, public authority, agency or another body, to which the personal data are disclosed, whether a third party or not. ...'

22. Under Article 6(1)(f) of that regulation:

'Processing shall be lawful only if and to the extent that at least one of the following applies:

...

(f) processing is necessary for the purposes of the legitimate interests pursued by the controller or by a third party, except where such interests are overridden by the interests or fundamental rights and freedoms of the data subject which require protection of personal data, in particular where the data subject is a child.'

23. Under Article 9 of that regulation:

'1. Processing of ... data concerning a natural person's sex life or sexual orientation shall be prohibited.

2. Paragraph 1 shall not apply if one of the following applies:

...

(f) processing is necessary for the establishment, exercise or defence of legal claims or whenever courts are acting in their judicial capacity;

(g) processing is necessary for reasons of substantial public interest, on the basis of Union or Member State law which shall be proportionate to the aim pursued, respect the essence of the right to data protection and provide for suitable and specific measures to safeguard the fundamental rights and the interests of the data subject;

...'

24. In accordance with Article 23(1)(i) and (j) of the same regulation:

> 'Union or Member State law to which the data controller or processor is subject may restrict by way of a legislative measure the scope of the obligations and rights provided for in Articles 12 to 22 and Article 34, as well as in Article 5 in so far as its provisions correspond to the rights and obligations provided for in Articles 12 to 22, when such a restriction respects the essence of the fundamental rights and freedoms and is a necessary and proportionate measure in a democratic society to safeguard:
>
> ...
>
> (i) the protection of the data subject or of the rights and freedoms of others;
>
> (j) the enforcement of civil law claims.'

25. Finally, Articles 94 and 95 of Regulation 2016/679 are worded as follows:

> 'Article 94
>
> Repeal of Directive [95/46]
>
> 1. Directive [95/46] is repealed with effect from 25 May 2018.
>
> 2. References to the repealed Directive shall be construed as references to this Regulation. ...

Article 95

Relationship with Directive [2002/58]

This Regulation shall not impose additional obligations on natural or legal persons in relation to processing in connection with the provision of publicly available electronic communications services in public communication networks in the Union in relation to matters for which they are subject to specific obligations with the same objective set out in Directive [2002/58].'

Examples of national legislation and case law

Denmark

Ophavsretsloven indeholder i §§ 76-80 også bestemmelser om straf i form af bøde for grovere immaterialretskrænkelser, der er begået forsætligt eller groft uagtsomt, jf. OHL § 76, stk. 1, og – for forsætlige overtrædelser begået under skærpende omstændigheder – fængselsstraf i op til et år og seks måneder, jf. OHL § 76, stk. 2. For overtrædelser af særlig grov karakter begået under særligt skærpende omstændigheder har straffelovens § 299 b skærpet strafferammen, så der kan idømmes fængselsstraf i op til 6 år.69 Juridiske personer kan idømmes bødestraf, jf. OHL § 80 med henvisning til straffelovens kap. 5. Strafansvaret kan gøres gældende efter reglen i straffelovens § 23 om medvirken til gerningen ved "tilskyndelse, råd eller dåd". Der vil oftest være tale om aktiv medvirken, men der er også eksempler i dansk retspraksis på idømmelse af straf for passiv medvirken.70 Det er naturligvis en betingelse, at tilregnelseskravet – forsæt eller grov uagtsomhed – er opfyldt.

69 Lovforslag L 55: Forslag til lov om ændring af straffeloven, retsplejeloven, markedsføringsloven og ophavsretsloven (IT-kriminalitet mv.), fremsat den 5. november 2003. Forslaget blev vedtaget ved lov nr. 352 af 19. maj 2004, og reglerne trådte i kraft den 1. juli 2004.

file:///C:/Users/Berna.000/Downloads/Speciale%204.pd
f

Translation:

Sections 76-80 of the Copyright Act also contain provisions on punishment in the form of fines for more serious infringements of intellectual property rights committed intentionally or grossly negligently, cf. OHL section 76, subsection 1, and – for intentional violations committed under aggravating circumstances – imprisonment for up to one year and six months, cf. OHL section 76, subsection 2. For offenses of a particularly serious nature committed under particularly aggravating circumstances, § 299 b of the Criminal Code has tightened the penalty framework, so that a prison sentence of up to 6 years can be imposed.69 Legal persons can be sentenced to a fine, cf. OHL § 80 with reference to the Criminal Code ch. 5. Criminal liability can be asserted according to the rule in Section 23 of the Criminal Code on complicity in the act by "incitement, advice or deed". This will most often be active complicity, but there are also examples in Danish jurisprudence of sentencing for passive complicity.70 It is of course a condition that the attribution requirement – intent or gross negligence – is met.

69 Bill L 55: Proposal for a law amending the Criminal Code, the Administration of Justice Act, the Marketing Act and the Copyright Act (IT crime, etc.), tabled on 5 November 2003. The proposal was adopted by Act No. 352 of 19 May 2004, and the rules came into force in force on 1 July 2004.

Case:

23. august 2021

Af Anette Pedersen

En mand er i dag ved Retten i Esbjerg dømt for ophavsretskrænkelser af særlig grov karakter.

En mand er i dag ved Retten i Esbjerg dømt for ophavsretskrænkelser af særlig grov karakter. Den dømte har ulovligt udbudt adgang til 21.000

ophavsretslige beskyttede værker, bestående af 9000 tv kanaler, 1000 sportskanaler og 11.000 film og serier igennem to hjemmesider med IPTV-tjenester (internet-tv). Gennem den ulovlige videreformidling har han omsat for ikke under 600.000 kroner.

Retten idømte manden fem måneders betinget fængsel, herunder betinget af 100 timers samfundstjeneste. Herudover blev den ulovlige fortjeneste og det anvendte udstyr konfiskeret.

Sagen blev indledt i maj 2020, hvor Statsadvokaten for Særlig Økonomisk og International Kriminalitet(SØIK) modtog en anmeldelse fra en rettighedshaver. Efter en indledende efterforskning ransagede SØIK den nu dømtes bopæl, og fandt blandt andet udstyr til re-transmission af tv-signaler, film og udsendelser.

Under retsmødet i dag erkendte manden, at han gennem en periode på halvandet år havde drevet de to hjemmesider, hvorfra det ulovlige IPTV blev udbudt, og at han sørgede for, at IPTV-tjenestens brugere fik adgang til de rettighedskrænkede værker. Hjemmesiderne havde en samlet omsætning på 600.000 kroner. Omsætningen blev genereret ved, at IPTV-tjenestens 450 brugere betalte for adgang til de 21.000 ophavsretsligt beskyttede værker gennem en abonnementsordning.

Hos Statsadvokaten for Særlig Økonomisk og International Kriminalitet(SØIK) er anklager Rasmus S. Hegelund tilfreds med dommen:

»Det er ulovligt at krænke ophavsretten, herunder at videreformidle tv uden rettighedshavers samtykke. Det er alvorlig kriminalitet, som ikke bare går ud over rettighedshaverne, men også den almindelige forbruger, som skal betale ekstra for sin lovlige adgang. Derfor har den dømte nu modtaget en straf for at have krænket en lang række rettighedshaveres ophavsret. Det er en skærpende omstændighed, at krænkelserne af ophavsretten er foregået i den størrelsesorden, som de er, og distribueret til så mange abonnenter, som der har været tale om,« siger Rasmus S. Hegelund.

https://anklagemyndigheden.dk/da/dom-grov-kraenkelse-af-ophavsretten

Translation:

23 August 2021

By Anette Pedersen

A man was sentenced today at the Court in Esbjerg for copyright infringements of a particularly serious nature.

A man was sentenced today at the Court in Esbjerg for copyright infringements of a particularly serious nature. The convict has illegally offered access to 21,000 copyright-protected works, consisting of 9,000 TV channels, 1,000 sports channels and 11,000 films and series through two websites with IPTV services (Internet TV). Through the illegal passing on, he has made sales of no less than DKK 600,000.

The court sentenced the man to five months' probation, including a condition of 100 hours of community service. In addition, the illegal profits and the equipment used were confiscated.

The case was initiated in May 2020, when the State Attorney for Special Economic and International Crime (SØIK) received a notification from a rights holder. After an initial investigation, SØIK searched the now convicted person's residence and found, among other things, equipment for re-transmission of TV signals, films and broadcasts.

During today's court hearing, the man admitted that, over a period of one and a half years, he had run the two websites from which the illegal IPTV was offered, and that he ensured that the users of the IPTV service had access to the infringed works. The websites had a total turnover of DKK 600,000. Revenue was generated by the IPTV service's 450 users paying for access to the 21,000 copyright-protected works through a subscription scheme.

At the State Attorney for Special Economic and International Crime (SØIK), prosecutor Rasmus S. Hegelund is satisfied with the verdict:

"It is illegal to infringe copyright, including broadcasting television without the rights holder's consent. It is serious crime, which not only affects the rights holders, but also the ordinary consumer, who has to pay extra for his legal access. Therefore, the convicted person has now received a punishment for infringing the copyright of a large number of rights holders. It is an aggravating circumstance that the infringements of copyright took place on the scale that they are, and distributed to as many subscribers as have been discussed,' says Rasmus S. Hegelund.

Luxembourg

Tribunal d'arrondissement de Luxembourg du 16 octobre 2014

Classements :

5.12.8.3 - DROIT ÉCONOMIQUE, COMMERCIAL ET FINANCIER - DROITS INTELLECTUELS - Droits d'auteur, droits voisins, bases de données - Droit d'auteur et droits voisins - Droit européen
4.1.2.9.2 - DROIT PÉNAL - CODE PÉNAL - Infractions et répression en particulier - Crimes et délits contre les propriétés (Art. 461 à 550) - Vols et extorsions (Art. 461 à 488)
4.1.2.9.3.8 - DROIT PÉNAL - CODE PÉNAL - Infractions et répression en particulier - Crimes et délits contre les propriétés (Art. 461 à 550) - Fraudes (Art. 489 à 509-7) - Infractions en matière informatique (Art. 509-1 à 509-7)
5.12.8.5 - DROIT ÉCONOMIQUE, COMMERCIAL ET FINANCIER - DROITS INTELLECTUELS - Droits d'auteur, droits voisins, bases de données - Base de

données - Droit européen
4.1.2.9.2.3 - DROIT PÉNAL - CODE PÉNAL - Infractions et répression en particulier - Crimes et délits contre les
propriétés (Art. 461 à 550) - Vols et extorsions (Art. 461 à 488) - Contrefaçon ou altération de clés (Art. 488)

droits voisins, bases de données - Base de données - Droit européen
4.1.2.9.2.3 - DROIT PÉNAL - CODE PÉNAL - Infractions et répression en particulier –

Crimes et délits contre les
propriétés (Art. 461 à 550) - Vols et extorsions (Art. 461 à 488) - Contrefaçon ou altération de clés (Art. 488)

Mots-clés :
vol nom d'accès, vol mot de passe, maintien frauduleux dans un système informatique, droits sur base de données

Références :
L00L0100000 A82 LOI
L00LC30 A509-1 CODE PENAL
L00L0100000 LOI
L00LC30 A461 CODE PENAL

Sommaire :
L'infraction de vol a été étendue dans son champ d'application par une loi du 18 juillet 2014. La loi pénale la plus
douce étant la loi pénale la plus restrictive, il convient d'appliquer en l'espèce l'article 461 du Code pénal dans sa
teneur applicable au moment des faits.
L'article 461 se lisait comme suit : « Quiconque a soustrait frauduleusement une chose qui ne lui appartient pas
est coupable de vol ».
Interprétation historique. L'approche historique ne permet que de tirer des conclusions limitées. Si les valeurs
immatérielles n'étaient pas entièrement inconnues à l'époque où l'infraction de vol a pris sa forme actuelle, elles ne
revêtaient cependant pas l'importance qu'elles ont actuellement.
Interprétation grammaticale. L'article 461 du Code pénal vise la « soustraction » d'une « chose », n'« appartenant
» pas à l'accusé. L'interprétation de la notion de « chose » doit se faire aussi au regard des notions d' «
appartenance » et de « soustraction ».
Vu le terme « appartenance », le vol ne peut porter que sur des choses susceptibles d'appartenir à quelqu'un.
L'appartenance, même à admettre qu'elle ne vise pas que le droit de propriété, doit pour le moins être un rapport

de droit qui établit un droit d'exclusivité univoque d'une personne sur cette « chose », donc un monopole
permettant d'exclure autrui de la jouissance de cette « chose ».
Ainsi, le vol ne saurait porter sur toute « information » quelconque, étant donné que les informations ne sont en
principe susceptibles ni d'appropriation (donc d'être l'objet d'un droit de propriété), ni d'appartenance. Ce n'est que
selon certains critères spécifiques, et en général avec un formalisme suppléant à la fonction que la possession

assume dans le monde tangible, que certaines informations peuvent devenir le monopole d'une personne
déterminée qui peut exercer sur elles des prérogatives exclusives proches d'un droit de propriété ; il s'agit des cas
de propriété intellectuelle, tels les droits d'auteur, droit de marques, brevets modèles et dessins, etc.

A part ces hypothèses, il n'existe pas de cadre législatif qui déterminerait à qui appartiennent des valeurs ou biens
incorporels et qui conféreraient un droit d'exclusivité.
En particulier, un mot de passe est éventuellement 'attribué' à une personne, mais il ne lui appartient pas. Dans la
logique de l'accusation, se poserait inévitablement la question de savoir si le docteur D.) était toujours en «
possession » du mot de passe ou si, en l'affichant à la vue d'un grand nombre de personnes, elle avait déjà perdu
toute emprise et tout monopole sur le code d'accès, de sorte que celui-ci était déjà « perdu » et ne pouvait donc
plus être « soustrait ».
Il faut encore constater qu'une « information » telle qu'un identifiant et un code d'accès, n'est pas susceptible de «
soustraction », notion qui suppose un appauvrissement (lat. sub-trahere ; sous-tirer, enlever par le bas). Or, le
Code d'accès était toujours à disposition du médecin. Suivre la logique de l'accusation amènerait à se poser la
question de savoir si X.) a volé deux fois la même chose, vu qu'il a pris deux photos du post-it. De manière plus
générale, une chose pourrait être volée à d'innombrables reprises à un même « propriétaire » sans que celui-ci

n'en soit dépossédé.
Comme l'a souligné le Conseil d'Etat, un vol d'informations ne saurait être assimilé d'office à une atteinte
patrimoniale : « il semble qu'il faille raisonner en cette matière plutôt en termes de possibilité d'atteinte
patrimoniale, alors que la captation illicite de données ou d'informations n'aura le plus souvent pas de portée
dommageable immédiate et effective, celle-ci n'étant le résultat que de l'usage qui sera fait des données et
informations illicitement captées » (Projet de loi n° 4641, Avis du Conseil d'Etat du 2 mai 2000, p. 20).
Pour le cas particulier des codes d'accès, il se pose également la question de savoir s'ils relèvent des « biens »
qui sont dans le commerce, ou si le mot de passe est plutôt à considérer comme un droit attaché à la personne.
Interprétation systématique. Le législateur étant supposé faire une œuvre cohérente, il y a également lieu
d'interpréter l'article 461 du Code pénal dans son contexte, c'est-à-dire au regard des autres normes de la
législation luxembourgeoise et de leur terminologie.
A ce titre, il y a lieu de constater que l'article 461 CP est le premier article du Titre IX intitulé « Crimes et délits

contre les propriétés ». Or, la propriété est une notion clairement définie et délimitée par notre législation ; elle
porte sur les « choses » (Art. 544 CCiv), qui est une notion moins vaste que celle de « bien » utilisée et détaillée
aux articles 516 et suivants du Code civil. L'ensemble de ces dispositions se caractérisent par une distinction
rigoureuse entre les « biens » et les « choses ».
S'il est vrai qu'en principe, le droit pénal jouit d'une certaine autonomie et que les concepts du droit civil ne
s'imposent pas rigoureusement lors de l'interprétation du droit pénal, il faut cependant constater que le Code pénal
a fait sienne la distinction terminologique entre les « choses » et les « biens » :
- L'article 505 sur le recel vise les « choses ou les biens incorporels »
- L'article 498 sur la tromperie précise que cette infraction s'applique « aux biens mobiliers y compris incorporels »
L'analyse terminologique des deux codes permet de constater que les « biens » visent une catégorie corporelle et
incorporelle, tandis que les « choses » se cantonnent au domaine du corporel.
Interprétation téléologique. La loi est l'expression de la volonté générale, exprimée dans son cadre constitutionnel
par le pouvoir législatif. Il convient dès lors de

l'appliquer en prenant en considération les intentions du législateur.
Lorsque les délits en matière informatique ont fait leur entrée dans notre législation, il avait été envisagé dans un premier temps d'adapter l'infraction de vol et de compléter l'article 461 du Code pénal comme suit : « Est assimilé au vol, le fait d'appréhender frauduleusement un bien immatériel ayant une valeur marchande appartenant à autrui en vue d'un usage ou emploi même momentané » (Projet de loi n° 4393 tendant à renforcer la lutte contre la criminalité économique et la fraude informatique, Texte du projet, page 2).
Le Conseil d'Etat a vivement critiqué cette approche et a jugé « préférable de créer des règles spéciales relatives à la fraude informatique » (Projet de loi n° 4393 précité, Avis du Conseil d'Etat, p. 14). Cette solution connaîtra la faveur du législateur, étant donné que l'article 461 restera inchangé et que les articles 509-1 et suivants du Code pénal ont été introduits par la loi du 15 juillet 1993 tendant à renforcer la lutte contre la criminalité économique et la
Parquet Général Service de documentation
Page 2

fraude informatique.
En 2000, les peines des infractions en matière informatiques ont été relevées sur base de la

considération
suivante (loi du 14 août 2000) :
« Le Conseil d'Etat propose toutefois un relèvement des pénalités encourues. Si la Chambre suit le Conseil d'Etat
dans sa proposition de ne pas envisager une répression de la fraude informatique au titre des incriminations
traditionnelles du vol, de l'extorsion, de l'abus de confiance et de l'escroquerie, les dispositions actuelles de l'article
509-1 du Code pénal permettant de l'appréhender, même si ce n'est que de manière indirecte, encore faut-il alors
prévoir des pénalités qui soient suffisamment dissuasives » (Projet de loi n° 4641/05 relatif au commerce
électronique, Rapport de la Commission de l'économie, de l'énergie, des postes et des transports du 10 juillet
2000, p. 30).
Le législateur s'était en effet laissé guider par l'idée que :
« les valeurs nouvelles que constituent les biens dits informationnels ou informatiques peuvent être l'objet
d'atteintes au même titre que les biens matériels traditionnels. Or, force est de constater que les infractions
classiques sanctionnant l'atteinte contre les biens, en particulier le vol, l'abus de confiance ou l'escroquerie, de
même que l'extorsion ou le recel, présupposent

la matérialité de l'objet du délit » (Projet de loi n° 4641, Exposé
des motifs, p. 28).
Par une loi postérieure aux faits reprochés à X.), le législateur a encore étendu la notion de vol qui peut désormais
porter sur « une chose ou une clef électronique ». Or, si dans l'intention du législateur, les choses englobaient
toutes les valeurs immatérielles, cette ajoute n'aurait pas été nécessaire.
Il découle de ce qui précède que le législateur n'a pas souhaité étendre le vol au-delà des biens matériels, mais a
préféré créer des infractions spécifiques.
A cela s'ajoute qu'admettre que le vol puisse couvrir toute information, voire même tout bien incorporel balayerait
encore la subtile gradation des peines mise en place par le législateur en matière d'atteinte à la propriété
intellectuelle, selon qu'elle affecte des droits d'auteur (simple amende ; Art. 82 de la loi modifiée du 18 avril 2011
sur les droits d'auteur, les droits voisins et les bases de données), des modèles ou des droits de marque (amende
et emprisonnement jusqu'à 3 ans, Art. 184 et 309 CP) ou des brevets (pas de sanction pénale).
Or, le législateur est supposé avoir fait une œuvre utile ; si aux yeux de la loi, toutes ces atteintes à des valeurs

immatérielles étaient de toute manière punies d'un emprisonnement de 5 ans à titre de vol, toutes les autres dispositions deviendraient inutile, superfétatoires et partant inopérantes. Or, rien ne permet d'admettre que le législateur ait voulu créer des dispositions inutiles, sombrant d'office dans les règles du concours avec le vol.
Par conséquent, le législateur a entendu la notion de « chose » comme ne visant que les biens matériels.
L'ensemble des considérations susmentionnées doivent encore être se mesurer au principe de l'interprétation stricte de la loi pénale, découlant du principe constitutionnel de la légalité des peines. Face aux incertitudes d'interprétation qui viennent d'être évoquées, l'interprétation la plus restrictive et donc la plus favorable au prévenu s'impose au juge pénal.
Le Tribunal constate par conséquent que l'infraction de vol ne saurait porter sur des biens incorporels, tels qu'en l'espèce des informations quant aux modalités d'accès à d'autres informations.
(...)
L'article 509-1 du Code pénal incrimine quiconque, frauduleusement, aura accédé ou se sera maintenu dans tout ou partie d'un système de traitement ou de transmission automatisé de données.

Les serveurs du CTIE, avec les bases de données qu'ils gèrent et les accès à distance qu'ils proposent, forment
un système de traitement et de transmission automatisé de données.
Il y a eu en l'espèce un accès, étant donné que le prévenu X.), en se servant de son ordinateur, a établi une
connexion avec les serveurs gérant la base de données SPMED, s'y est connecté et a lancé différentes requêtes.
Quant à la notion de « maintien », il convient de constater que celle-ci « vise à sanctionner l'auteur qui aurait
accédé de bonne foi et par inadvertance à un système informatique sans disposer de l'autorisation nécessaire puis
Parquet Général Service de documentation
Page 3

se serait maintenu dans ledit système après avoir eu conscience du caractère illicite de l'intrusion » (LEROUX
Olivier, Criminalité informatique, in : Les infractions contre les biens, Larcier 2008, p. 414).
En l'espèce, X.) est « resté » sur le site, après avoir accédé de manière non autorisée, il ne s'est pas « maintenu »
après un accès autorisé ; le « maintien » ne peut dès lors être retenu à sa charge.
Quant à l'élément moral, l'article 509-1 exige outre le dol général également un dol spécial, à savoir que l'accès

doit avoir été fait « frauduleusement », donc dans une intention frauduleuse. En l'espèce, X.) savait qu'il n'était pas
habilité à accéder à la base de données en question et s'est néanmoins volontairement connecté ; il a dès lors agi
dans une intention frauduleuse. Le mobile sous-jacent au passage à l'acte est à ce titre indifférent et ne rend pas
l'accès légitime.
(...)
Atteinte aux droits sur base de données. Dans son ordonnance, la Chambre du conseil entend voir les faits
qualifiés d'infraction à l'article 82 de la loi modifiée du 18 avril 2011 sur les droits d'auteur, les droits voisins et les
bases de données.
Le prédit article incrimine notamment « quiconque, sciemment, vend, offre en vente, importe, exporte, fixe,
reproduit, communique, transmet par fil ou sans fil, met à la disposition du public et de manière générale, met ou
remet en circulation, à titre onéreux ou gratuit ... une base de données sans autorisation ... du producteur de base
de données ».
La législation sur la propriété intellectuelle protège sous certaines conditions des créations de l'esprit en conférant
un monopole ; elle accorde notamment aux producteurs de bases de données un droit

qualifié de « sui generis ».
Sont des bases de données, « les recueils ou complications d'œuvres ou d'autres éléments indépendants,
disposés de manière systématique ou méthodique et individuellement accessibles par des moyens électroniques
ou d'une autre manière » (Art. 1 (2) de la loi du 18 avril 2011).
En l'espèce, les données du SPMED forment une compilation d'éléments indépendants accessibles par des
moyens électroniques, et donc une base de données au sens de la prédite loi.
La base de données SPMED est constamment mise à jour, de sorte que le délai de protection de 15 ans (Art. 69
de la loi du 18 avril 2011) n'a pas encore expiré.
L'article 67 (3) al. 3 de la loi précise que « pour autant qu'elles soient licitement rendues publiques, les bases de
données appartenant à l'Etat peuvent être copiées dans leur intégralité dans les conditions fixées par règlement
grand-ducal » ; ledit règlement grand-ducal n'a pas encore été pris. En l'espèce, la base de données SPMED a été
licitement rendue accessible à un certain nombre d'usagers (les médecins et leurs assistants), mais n'est pas
accessible au grand public. Cette exception ne trouve dès lors pas application en l'espèce.

La base de données SPMED est partant une base de données relevant du monopole de son producteur.
Comme producteur, il y a lieu de considérer « la personne physique ou morale qui prend l'initiative et assume à
titre principal le risque d'effectuer les investissements nécessaires à la création d'une base de données » (Art. 67
(2) de la loi du 18 avril 2011).
Le service médico-sportif est organisé par le ministre ayant le sport dans ses attributions (Règlement grand-ducal
du 8 février 2012 concernant le contrôle médico-sportif obligatoire des membres licenciés actifs des fédérations
sportives agréées ; le règlement grand-ducal du 26 août 1980, applicable au moment des faits, retient le même
principe). Les Ministères n'ayant pas de personnalité morale propre, il y a lieu de considérer l'Etat comme étant le
producteur de la base de données SPMED.
Il n'y a eu en l'espèce aucun accord de la part de l'Etat pour que X.) accède à la base de données SPMED.
L'article 82 précité n'incrimine pas la simple consultation non autorisée d'une base de données.
En l'espèce, X.) a enregistré diverses données sur ses propres supports informatiques et a envoyé ces données
par courrier électronique au vice-président du

parti pirate.
Il y a par conséquent eu une opération de « reproduction », de « communication », de « transmission par fil et
sans fil » et de « mise en circulation ».
Cet acte doit avoir porté sur une « base de données ». En l'espèce, ont été enregistrés et transmis :
- un fichier représentant l'électrocardiogramme de X.)
-quatorze (14) captures d'écran (Screenshot).
Le Tribunal constate que 13 fichiers se rapportent exclusivement à
Parquet Général Service de documentation
Page 4

la fiche de X.). La dernière est un extrait de l'agenda du service médico-sportif.
Or, tel que détaillé ci-avant, la base de données se définit comme étant une « compilation d'éléments
indépendants ». Si un sous-ensemble d'une base de données peut à son tour être une base de données, l'extrait
tiré d'une seule fiche de la base de données, ou des éléments simplement isolés ne constituent pas en soi une
base de données. Les screenshots ne sont pas non plus « disposés de manière systématique », ni «
individuellement accessibles ».
Les informations que X.) a enregistrées et distribuées ne constituent donc pas une « base de données » en soi, tel

que l'exige l'article 82 de la loi du 18 avril 2011.
Parquet Général Service de documentation
Page 5

https://www.stradalex.lu/fr/slu_src_publ_jur_lux/document/ecli_lu_tal_2014_02628-1016

Austria

Any person who commits an infringement of the kind referred to in section 86, paragraph 1; section 90b; section 90c, paragraph 1; or section 90d, paragraph 1 of the Copyright Act shall be liable to imprisonment not exceeding six months or to a fine not exceeding 360 times the daily rate; 'daily rate' means the unit for the calculation of the fine on a certain daily basis. Therefore, Austrian verdicts determine a certain number of such daily rates and the respective amount for these rates. For instance, if the defendant is sentenced to 180 daily rates at €70, the fine in total amounts to €12,600. The infringement shall not, however, be punishable if it only involves the unauthorised reproduction or an unauthorised recording of a recitation or a performance for personal use or for the personal use of another person, effectively free of charge

https://www.lexology.com/library/detail.aspx?g=294cc960-601d-4948-b018-fda672aeab20

Spain

Criminal proceedings for copyright are regulated by the Criminal Procedure Act (Royal decree of 14 September 1882). Crimes related to copyright are
established in Articles 270, 271, and 272 of the Criminal Code (organic act 10/1995, of 23 November) (*Código Penal*) as modified by:

- Law 5/2010, of 22 June, regarding penalty schemes for retail distribution.
- Law 1/2015, of 22 March, amending the Criminal Code.

https://uk.practicallaw.thomsonreuters.com/w-011-1027?transitionType=Default&contextData=(sc.Default)

Unlike U.S. law, where criminal charges are brought only by a government prosecutor, Spanish law allows ordinary citizens to pursue criminal actions by filing criminal complaints. If a victim files a complaint directly with an instructing (or investigative) judge, the victim becomes a party in the case during the investigation and trial phases. This is known as a private prosecution or *acusación particular*. Spanish law also allows people not directly connected to the crime to take part in the case. Important public interest groups often join these complaints as popular prosecutors or *acusadores populares*.

The criminal division (of the Spanish National Court) is made up of six chambers. An instructing judge presides over each chamber. For example, well-known Judge Baltasar Garzón has for many years been the presiding judge in charge of Chamber Number 5. Once an instructing judge accepts a criminal case, he or she initiates an investigation that can take anywhere from 30 days to several years. After this investigation phase is concluded, the instructing judge closes the case and transfers it to a tribunal – normally a panel with three judges – that will preside over the trial, known as the "oral phase" of the case. Under Spanish criminal law, no defendant can be tried in absentia.

In 1985 Spain passed an Organic Law that defined the jurisdiction of Spanish courts in criminal cases. The law gave Spanish courts jurisdiction in several kinds of cases, such as when the criminal act took place on Spanish soil or when the perpetrator of the crime is of Spanish nationality.

Additionally, the new law gave Spanish courts jurisdiction over cases related to a particular type of international crimes - ones that are of international concern - regardless of the nationality of the perpetrator or where the crime took place. This section of the law incorporates the principle of "universal jurisdiction" - the principle that certain crimes are so egregious that they are offenses against the entire world and can therefore be tried in the national courts of any country. Some of these crimes were listed in the law, including genocide, terrorism and piracy. A residual clause also grants jurisdiction for "any other [criminal act] which, according to international covenants and treaties, should be prosecuted in Spain." It has been argued that this residual clause incorporates the offenses of torture and crimes against humanity.

The principle of universal jurisdiction is not particular to Spain. International treaties, including the Geneva Conventions and the Convention Against Torture, permit and, in some cases, require nations to prosecute perpetrators of egregious human rights abuses even if those nations have no connection to the crimes. Until recently however, the principle of universal jurisdiction was largely aspirational, an ideal discernible in bodies of international law, but lacking in concrete precedent.

This changed dramatically in 1996, when instructing judges from the SNC invoked the new Spanish law to begin investigating human rights cases arising from the 'Dirty War' era in Argentina and Pinochet dictatorship in Chile. The Argentine cases involved the investigation of some 100 suspects. The Chilean cases focused on former dictator Augusto Pinochet and his subordinates. The case against Pinochet in Spain, and his arrest in England based on an extradition request from Spain, launched the modern concept of universal jurisdiction and opened the door to the exercise of universal jurisdiction over human rights crimes by national courts.

https://cja.org/what-we-do/litigation/legal-strategy/the-spanish-national-court/

Amazon warehouse workers at four Amazon warehouses on Staten Island rallied outside the National Labor Relations Board and hand-carried four plastic containers filled with signed cards into a local labor office, petitioning it to authorize a union vote. 25 Oct 2021. Image: Myotus

Appeal

To buy or not to buy – the essential question!

The authors ask you, the general public, not to buy counterfeit goods or works.

Even if the price is tantalizing.

We acknowledge this is a huge temptation especially if you have a small budget.

But consider for a moment that you don´t in any way support the authors by buying a counterfeit book via Amazon or one of their "trusted sellers" – or anyone else.

You may only support Jeff Bezos´ quest to become the richest man in the World.

Please buy the legal version.

If you desire a better quality than the legal paperback, please visit a large national chain of book sellers in the USA.

They have a "secret" database with our books in hardback – or most of them. But you have to be rather insistent to be get them to access this "secret" database". We don´t know why.

Alternatively, you can support us directly.

In the US it takes us abt $2.000.00 to make a printed version in a good quality available that you can then buy via Amazon.

In the EU it will be a bit more because we have to take a first print run of 50 books. Maybe you can even sell them for us?

Please support us by buying the legal versions so that we can write and publish more books.

Thank you and God Bless!

Made in United States
North Haven, CT
04 November 2026

21727487R00257